Get a Life!

the guide book

Get a Life!

the guide book

Lisa Whitehead

Winchester, UK
Washington, USA

First published by O-Books, 2012
O-Books is an imprint of John Hunt Publishing Ltd., Laurel House, Station Approach,
Alresford, Hants, SO24 9JH, UK
office1@jhpbooks.net
www.johnhuntpublishing.com

For distributor details and how to order please visit the 'Ordering' section on our website.

Text copyright: Lisa Whitehead 2012

ISBN: 978 1 78099 388 1

All rights reserved. Except for brief quotations in critical articles or reviews, no part of this book may be reproduced in any manner without prior written permission from the publishers.

The rights of Lisa Whitehead as author have been asserted in accordance with the Copyright, Designs and Patents Act 1988.

A CIP catalogue record for this book is available from the British Library.

Design: Stuart Davies

Printed in the USA by Edwards Brothers Malloy

We operate a distinctive and ethical publishing philosophy in all areas of our business, from our global network of authors to production and worldwide distribution.

CONTENTS

Introduction

Thank you for picking up this little book from the book shelf. Congratulations, you've made a wise choice. This book may not be the biggest or the thickest book on the shelf, but don't underestimate what it will do for you. If you're holding it in your hands, then be sure it has chosen you to work with, and not the other way around. Everything happens for a reason, even if not apparent at the time. As you will learn as we travel on your journey through this book, you will at some point have drawn this little book towards you, and that is why without doubt you're reading these words now.

This book came to manifestation as a result of an intent I put out sometime ago. In order to bring it to fruition I have been on a long journey to Get a Life! myself. You see, in order to write these words I had to wake up!

That's right, wake up!

Maybe you've done it yourself, you're drifting along through life, day after day, and showing up to life just as you did yesterday. Then it happens...sometimes it's a gentle nudge, a fleeting thought... "There must be more to life than this" or "Is this it? Is this all there is?" or for others it hits like a sledgehammer or demolition ball...shaking you to your very core.

For me it was I guess a few nudges to begin with, but I simply didn't listen, I kept on doing what I did in the same way I'd always done, thinking that's just what you do. But when the universe calls to your spirit and you don't listen, then it calls again and if you still don't listen; as was the case in my journey, then it shouts at the top of its voice for you to wake up, my shout came in the form of severe post-natal depression after the birth of my beautiful daughter Sarah, over 18 years ago, followed by M.E. (*myalgic encephalomyelitis*). Crazy but true…It took a debilitating illness to make me wake up to my spirit's call!

Many years down the line, I have been on a long and life-transforming journey of which I'm truly grateful, I might add. My journey has taken me through the wonders of complementary therapy, letting go of my old corporate career, developing my spirituality, a divorce, ups and downs and rounds and rounds, until I was ready to write this little book and in turn help others.

Today, I'm wide awake, in perfect health, blissfully happy with myself, my life, the love of my life, Jon, my wonderful daughter (who has taught me so much and continues to do so), my loving family (now much extended to include Jon's lovely girls, Olivia and Rachel) and my wonderful friends...I have become a very different human being to the old Lisa. I have evolved. Before I was all about "doing" now I'm about "being". The gift I was given, my wake-up call, allowed me to follow my true calling. In order that I can now live on purpose. I Got a Life!

I hope that this little book may bring you great pleasure and allow you to wake up gently, bringing your true spirit to light.

Namaste
Lisa x

Author's note

How to use this book:
I have written this book in just the same way I write my blog, in that it has flowed just as a theme and thought came to me. You can read it from the first page to the last. But equally you can open it at any chapter and read that passage for the day and complete the suggested exercise that accompanies it. Your intuition will guide you. You will read what you most need at that particular time, as I always say, "The universe works in mysterious and miraculous ways!" Trust that your spirit will bring the messages in this book to you in perfect timing.

1

Nurturing your space

Well, what a great start to the day, I've spent all morning doing the housework. And do you know what, it's been an absolute joy!

Really, I'm serious, I've savoured every moment of it. Incense burning, uplifting music and a time to really nurture our home. Don't you feel that sometimes we can all get too busy with life, the hustle and bustle, the running around with an endless "To do" list in hand, to really take the time to nurture our environment. Be it our home or our workplace, really it's just an outer display; a representation of what's going on with our own inner space.

I love tending to the nurturing of our home, as in turn it's nurturing myself and those I love around me. This morning I took great pleasure in going out into the garden to cut some fresh yellow roses, growing at the front of our home, I choose them for the vase in the hallway, right at the entrance to our home. So now when we return home from our busy lives, we are welcomed by the freshness of the beautiful, fragrant yellow buds breaking into bloom...Mmm let's think about that for a moment. If our environment is displaying what's going on, on the inside of us, then my yellow roses are encouraging the growth of confidence, knowledge, self-esteem, authenticity and personal power, as the buds open to bloom then perhaps all of these aspects of myself and my loved ones are also beginning to bloom!

As you will grow to learn throughout this book, I always look for the meaning and symbolism in everything that I notice around me. If I become aware of these symbols and signs around me, I have a greater connection to all that is and the web and strands that connect everyone and everything. The clues are there if you just open your eyes enough to see.

I had a long discussion with a good friend of mine just a few days ago about the energy of nurture. It doesn't matter if you're male or female, the feminine energy of nurture is so important to our growth as spiritual beings having a human experience. We can so easily take for granted at times, the importance of expressing this energy. For me it can be something as simple as taking pleasure in doing the housework, knowing that I am lovingly nurturing our home and therefore ourselves.

In simple terms, if we do not nurture our environment, our homes and ourselves we don't have the capacity to grow. Just in the same way a gardener nurtures their seedlings, or a parent nurtures their child...Nurture is imperative for growth!

Taking time to review your own space can uncover so many opportunities for nurturing your growth. Have you noticed that when your environment is cluttered your mind feels cluttered as well?

If your bedroom is unloved and uncared for, have you noticed that no matter how much sleep you have you wake feeling un-refreshed?

There really is positive uplifting energy to be had by doing the housework, clearing the weeds in the garden and emptying the washing basket, it's true!

Exercise - Nurturing your space.

Stop and take a look around you wherever you are right now. You may be in your car, in your office, working at your desk, or somewhere in your home.

What do you notice?

Take a moment now to reflect on how your outer nurturing reflects your inner nurturing, note down your observations.

Where does your space require more nurture?

What does this reflect within you?

What action will you take right now, today, to nurture your space and in turn yourself?

Once you've completed your nurturing, capture how it makes you feel.

2

Fantastic Day!

I saw the title of the 80s band *Haircut 100* song "Fantastic Day!" Quoted in my friend's facebook status this morning, it took me back to being a teenager, such a great song, with lots of feel-good memories!

I decided to search out the video on You Tube...As I watched the beginning of video, it shows the band imprisoned and unhappy in a prison cell, then it shows how easily they can simply, and with little effort, push down the walls that contain them and be free.

It made me think.

How many times do we put up false walls, feeling we're trapped, stuck or are prevented in some way of being free?

Often, just like in the video, we're simply a prisoner of our own limiting beliefs and thoughts. We are the sum of all that we have thought until this point. Our unconscious mind stores all of the information and data, we have carefully filed in our "inner filing cabinet" to be referred to at any given moment in the future. Conditioning that we have received from a lifetime of experiences. Our unconscious mind stores all of those beliefs with attached emotional responses in our inner filing cabinet regardless of if it still holds true. Basically it can't tell fact from fiction. The great news is every moment is the opportunity for a new beginning! We can choose our thoughts, we can choose the emotional response we attach to them and in turn this will change our outward experience.

So often we forget this, we keep going back to the inner filing cabinet, pulling out the same old file and forget that we have a choice, so in effect we keep ourselves imprisoned – when in truth even if in the worst-case scenario our body were imprisoned, our mind and spirit are always free. There is always a choice.

For most of us thankfully we have our liberty and freedom, but do we consider ourselves free spirits?

Or do we allow ourselves to feel trapped by our circumstances, be it our relationships, our work, our family responsibilities or our finances.

Yes we all have responsibility – the ability to choose our response.

Exercise - Unlocking the spirit

Take a moment to consider- Where in your life do you limit your freedom to be all that you can be?

What really restricts you from having a "Fantastic Day" today and every day?

What truly holds you back, what locks you in?

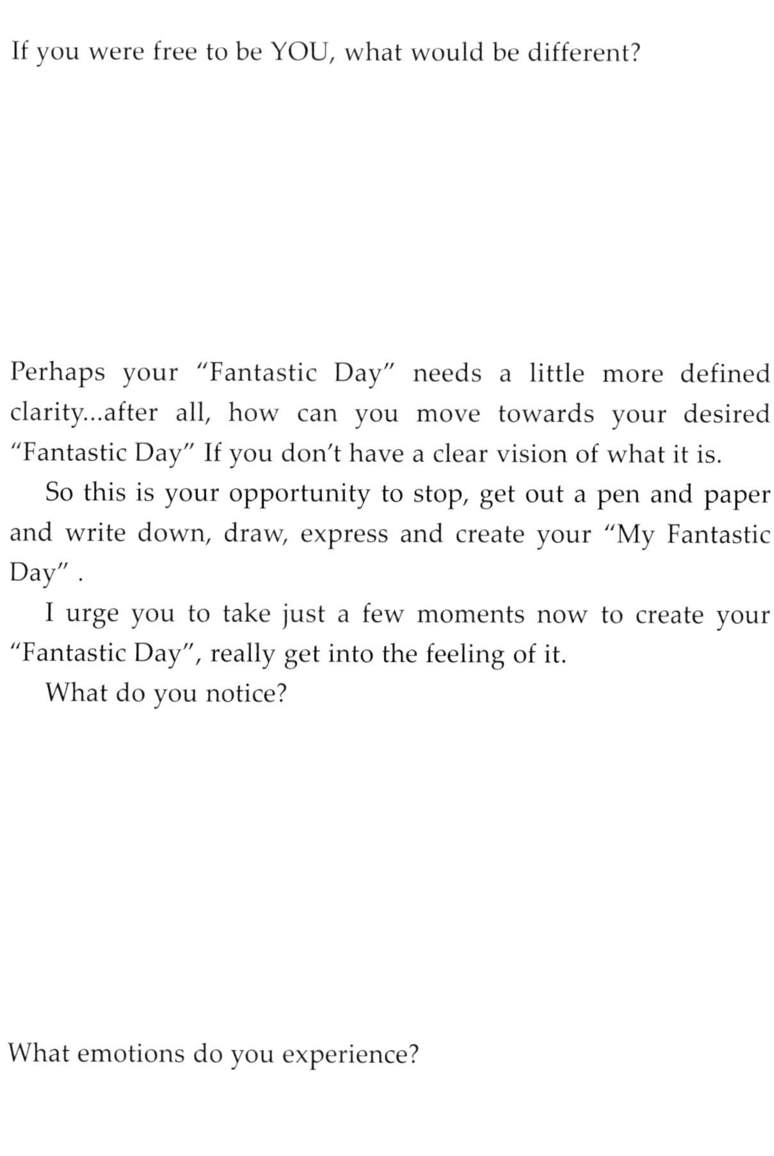

If you were free to be YOU, what would be different?

Perhaps your "Fantastic Day" needs a little more defined clarity...after all, how can you move towards your desired "Fantastic Day" If you don't have a clear vision of what it is.

So this is your opportunity to stop, get out a pen and paper and write down, draw, express and create your "My Fantastic Day" .

I urge you to take just a few moments now to create your "Fantastic Day", really get into the feeling of it.

What do you notice?

What emotions do you experience?

What exactly is your "Fantastic Day"? Examine every juicy detail, imagine it right now in glorious Technicolor. Note what you can see, feel, hear, touch, taste.

Are you surprised?

When I pose this type of question to most people, they really want something that is just within reach! And it's something totally available to them with just a few changes to their thoughts (and a few re-filing activities in the inner filing cabinet).

Now you have got a clear picture of your "Fantastic Day" you can consider:

What is currently taking you further away from your "Fantastic Day"?

What would take you closer toward it?

What imprisoning beliefs are holding you back that you can let go of right now?

Have a FANTASTIC DAY!

A man will be imprisoned in a room with a door that's unlocked and opens inwards; as long as it does not occur to him to pull rather than push
~ Ludwig Wittgenstein

3

Happy Talk!

How do you talk, I mean how do you speak to others and to yourself?

If you were to consider how much of your talk is happy talk, what would you say?

We can all too easily get caught up in the moaning and groaning of ourselves and others, taking on negative media, watching negative television coverage, but how aware are you of what you're focusing on?

How much of it is happy talk?

It's true that where focus goes energy flows, so the more you focus on happy talk the more your energy will move in that direction, flowing to more happiness and allowing more happy talk to flow towards you.

If we consider the wonderful words from South Pacific...

Happy talkin', talkin Happy talk
Talk about things you'd like to do
You've got to have a dream
If you don't have a dream
How you gonna have a dream come true

Why not try this today.....

Focus your energy on your dreams, be inspired and inspiring, let your talk be happy...because what you focus on is what is drawn towards you, where your thoughts and talk go is where your energy flows and that's what will manifest in your reality...

I'd urge you not to get caught up in the confusion and doubt that may be the chatter going on around you. Instead I'd urge you to start a change yourself...be the leader of the "Happy Talk" change today.

Life still goes on, the moon will still shine tonight, the birds were still singing this morning, the World keeps on turning...Your dreams are still your dreams...What you focus on is what counts...Sing to your own tune today...I urge you to make it a happy one.

Why not actively make a choice to have fun today?

Know that your sparkling hopes and dreams are still within your grasp...reach for the stars, you are limitless.

In truth the only restrictions you truly have are those you carry in your heart.

Not only that YOU can start a ripple...you can start the "Happy Talk" today!

We can all find something in our lives to make Happy Talk about. Even if you're going through a really difficult time right now, by focusing your attention on even the smallest thing that you can be happy about, you can expand that energy, simply by focusing on it.

Exercise – Happy talk

How lucky and blessed are you today? Take a moment to list as many things in your life that you feel blessed with.

What can you give thanks for? What are you grateful for in your life today?

Today I urge you to notice how you talk, to yourself and to others, keep your attention on only speaking happy talk today. If you find yourself talking anything but happy talk, stop take a breath, acknowledge and let go, then simply return to happy talk.

At the end of the day capture your thoughts and feeling of your happy talk today. What do you notice?

Each new day is a day to be lived.
Will you talk happily today?
Will you draw more "Happy Talk" into your awareness?
Wishing you lots of HAPPY TALK today!

4

Make a wish!

This is a magical moment, this moment right NOW!

I urge you to stop what you're doing and consider this...

What one positive wish would you wish for right now?

As children we made wishes all the time, blowing out candles on our birthday cake, blowing on dandelion heads, watching the seeds spread far and wide, carrying with them our wishes.

Magical manifestation was never in question as a child. With all our heart we would blow breath and life into our wishes. So why then as adults do we stop?

We all have hopes, wishes and desires, but as adults we can almost get in our own way of manifesting them. Maybe we don't feel we deserve our wishes, maybe we can't believe that our wishes coming true could be possible. Maybe we don't allow ourselves to dream, for fear of being disappointed.

Well, today I'm being your fairy godmother, I'm giving you permission to dream. Right now I'm asking you to make a wish and allow the magic to occur. Of course it's important that your wish is positive, that you feel worthy and deserving of receiving it and it needs to be something you can believe can actually be real.

So, here's your chance...

Exercise - Make a wish

Make a wish...state right now your desire...phrase it as if it were already real, step into the manifestation of it, try it on for size.

What does it feel like to have this wish come true?

Feel it in the very heart of you!

Do you feel the excitement and joy, describe how it feels.

How are you different, now your wish has come true, what do you notice?

Describe how great is life now your wish has come true?

Now feel grateful for this wish coming true, appreciate every little piece of it! Give thanks for it!

Now comes the magic...ask your inner guide (I like to call it "my bright spark") to show you when opportunities come up that take you towards your wish...Ask for that nudge when the moment comes to follow and take action...Every step is a step closer to your wish!

And now, simply let it go!

Just like blowing out the candles on a cake or the seeds on a dandelion head, let your wish drift out on the wind!

The magic is already happening!

Breathe life into your wildest dreams...may your wishes come true!

"Somewhere over the rainbow, skies are blue, and the dreams that you dare to dream really do come true"

5

Shine on

A smile is the light in your window that tells others that there is a caring, sharing person inside. ~ Denis Waitley

This chapter took a while to write...Mainly due to the fact I couldn't remember the name of the song my head kept on playing to me.

But thanks to the good old internet and the help of my friends, I eventually found the song that had been running around on repeat on my inner music system, which led to the writing of this chapter.

Anyway, I had already written my chapter for today...Make a wish...but I felt compelled to write this one too.

It struck me that we sometimes underestimate how much we can touch others at the heart of them in the simplest ways, by simply sharing our light. By that I mean sharing our uplifting thoughts, a smile, a kind word...our positivity and support.

We all have a flame within us, for some that flame burns bright, in others it may just be a tiny spark...but it's there...always...

You know when you're having a bad day, you know one of those really awful days when you just want to curl up under the duvet and not face the world????

Have you noticed that it only takes a friend or a loved one to smile at you, praise you, appreciate you...shine their light on you and even the most difficult situations, somehow seem lighter...more bearable...allowing you to embrace the day, whatever may come.

By sharing your light, you can light the way for those that are in less brightness than yourself. When you share your light you never know just how many candles you're lighting along the way!

Even when we're having the best day...Have you noticed as human beings we're naturally drawn to those whose light shines brightly?

Somehow they just exude warmth, you naturally want to gravitate towards them!

So today I urge you to "shine on" let the light of love shine on......

Exercise: Shine on

Ask yourself: How can you brighten someone else's day today?

Record your experiences of sharing your light:

6

Don't give up!

As I picked my guidance card of the day this morning – "Have Faith", I received a "Tweet" from a good friend who said she had just pulled her card for the day – "Trust". I decided today to write about not giving up!

As Peter Gabriel sings, in the song "Don't Give Up" – *"It is so strange the way things turn"* sometimes life throws us a curve ball when we're least expecting it!

Whilst thinking about the topic of "Don't Give Up" I was reminded of a quote from Harriet Beecher Stowe the American abolitionist and author.

"Never give up, for that is just the place and time that the tide will turn".

It is at that point when we may think," What's the point?" that we let go, we surrender. By surrender I don't mean chucking in the towel exactly, I mean allowing ourselves to be open to grace...when we think, "I give up" it's often the moment that we may be closest to the breakthrough we're looking for!

I'm not saying that its always easy to "have faith" or "trust" as the cards of the day suggested, sometimes it takes real effort to remain true to our positive thoughts...but thoughts as we've already mentioned do become things. So by focusing on the negative, by bringing your attention to lack, the universe has no choice but to respond accordingly, bringing more negativity and lack into your awareness, the superconscious mind has to deliver that to you, as an act of preserving sanity!

So no matter what curveballs may come your way today, rise above them. Focus on all the things you're grateful for, even noticing the very smallest thing you're grateful for, will shift your focus away from "Giving up" then just...

Start by doing what's necessary;
then do what's possible;
and suddenly you are doing the impossible

A great piece of advice from St.Francis of Assisi. Worrying never solved a problem, but positive attitude and positive action sure will take the momentum out of any hurtling curve ball!

Albert Einstein gives these three pointers:

1. Out of clutter, find simplicity.
2. From discord, find harmony.
3. In the middle of difficulty lies opportunity.

I know you may be thinking it's all well and good for you Lisa, you're Miss Positivity personified...well even positivity experts have those curveballs fly at them from time to time!

Life has to give you experiences in equal measure, you may call it the good with the bad, the ups with the downs, it's all part of the journey...without the awareness of what we don't want, how can we identify and manifest what we do?

So I urge you today, if there's any area in your life where you feel like "giving up"...Don't take my advice; take the wise words gifted to you by the greats!

St.Francis and Albert...

Exercise: Don't give up

Consider what is cluttering your life, what no longer serves you? (People, situations, things)

Which of these are you willing to simply "let go" of?

What would make your life more simple right now?

What feels discordant in your life right now?

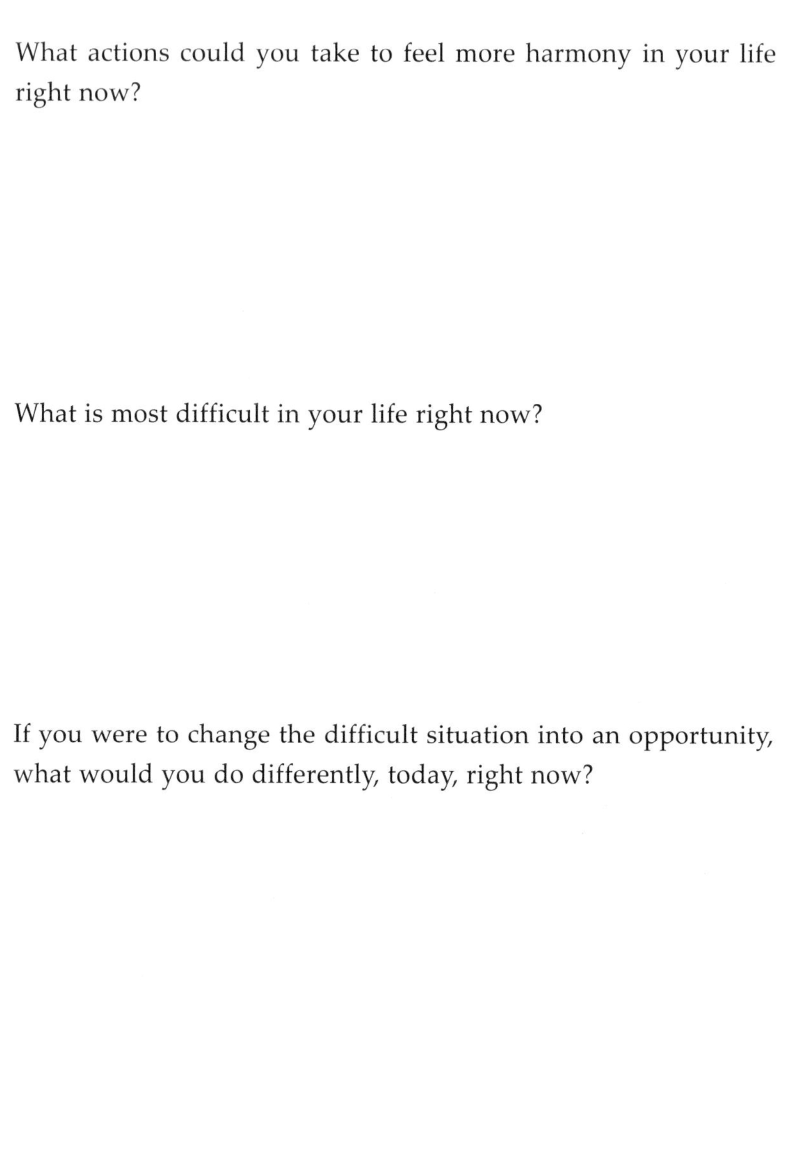

What actions could you take to feel more harmony in your life right now?

What is most difficult in your life right now?

If you were to change the difficult situation into an opportunity, what would you do differently, today, right now?

7

It's the contrast that counts

It's been exceptionally hot over the past weekend, seasonally way above average temperatures for May at 28 degrees. I love the warm weather, waking up to the sun streaming in through the windows as I wake and hearing the birdsong to welcome the day. However, today, Wednesday, all has changed, it's probably not even 14 degrees...the sun isn't shining...as I look out through my kitchen window, the skies are grey.

But, what stands out to me is the contrasting bright yellow field below, the rape seed in the farmer's field directly behind my garden glows so brightly against the grey backdrop of the sky it looks almost surreal...so beautiful, so vibrant.

It was only because of the contrast that I could truly see its beauty!

It got me to thinking...life is full of contrast...We may label it; hot and cold, up and down, good and bad, happy and sad...but in truth if there were no contrast, how could we appreciate the beauty?

It's in the contrast that the true gift is revealed.

What would an artist capture without the gift of contrast?

Have you ever tried to adjust the contrast on your TV?

Turn up or down the contrast and what happens? ...Exactly, the picture disappears! It cannot be seen!

Contrast is the point of clarity between opposites. To appreciate all experiences in life, it is the contrast that makes it possible. So when you hear those around you complaining that it's "too hot" or "too cold", I urge you to help them see that it's the contrast that counts.

Imagine if there were no contrast...There would be no life!

Celebrate the contrast, be it in people, cultures, beliefs, personalities, situations, environments...Wherever and whenever contrast shows up, remember, it's the colourful palette that makes the painting of the picture of life so very colourful!

Every act of creation is first an act of destruction
~ Pablo Picasso

Exercise: notice the contrast

Today, note down the contrast that you notice around you, be it a different point of view, or maybe a different belief, any contrast can allow us growth, so becoming aware of the contrast allows us the opportunity to learn.

8

Beautifully Unique!

unique
adj.
1. Being the only one of its kind.
2. Without an equal or equivalent; unparalleled.
3. *Informal* Unusual; extraordinary.
4. *Informal* very remarkable or unusual.

Do you feel beautifully unique?

When I was considering what to write about in today's chapter, I flicked through one of my favourite books, which happened to be close to hand, I stopped at a page and just read, *"I must believe my own abilities and worth"*. I stopped to consider the message in this for myself and for everyone that might find themselves reading this book. As I read on I became quite uplifted and excited...

(Being that I am a beautifully unique, tree-hugging nut...who loves to live life with simple gratitude and a passion for positivity!)

As we spoke of earlier you are the sum total and accumulation of all that you have experienced so far.

But this is just where you're at now in your journey, the road leads out ahead of you, far ahead, onto the horizon, beyond that horizon will be another and another, and you haven't even begun to imagine them yet!

Wow, how very exciting is that? How many potential choices and opportunities are ahead of you, just waiting for you to choose.

How amazing, we – you and I – can choose in every moment where the path goes, our choices are unique to us, only you can tread your steps and only I can tread mine!

The passage in my favourite book went on to talk about throwing a dart at a map, the chances of landing in exactly the same place twice would be very unlikely. Just like us, each of us individual, with our unique combination of character, skills, dreams, wishes...even an identical twin, who may look the same as their sibling is in fact; in truth, beautifully unique!

We may appear similar, we may tread similar paths, but in truth we cannot ever measure our uniqueness against another. We are gorgeously different, one of a kind, bringing our unique gifts to all that we meet.

I urge you to take a moment now to write down all the things that make YOU beautifully unique...

No one smiles as you do, no one laughs quite like you, no one has those funny little quirky pieces of loveliness that make you – YOU!

All too often we measure ourselves against others in a negative way, belittling our own abilities and worth. A good friend of mine calls it "comparing and despairing".

My challenge to you is this...During today make an effort to notice the unique value you bring to the World by being YOU!

No one else can step into the space that you fill, they're not you....

You can't be anyone else...because they're all already taken!

Celebrate BEAUTIFUL UNIQUENESS today in yourself and in others...notice those people who walk alongside you, your loved ones, friends and colleagues...Be brave share with them what you find beautifully unique about them!

Exercise: Beautifully unique

Today I urge you to comment on what makes you BEAUTIFULLY UNIQUE.

Feel proud to share your uniqueness with the World today and celebrate the wonder that is YOU!

9

Will you do something amazing today?

Everyone's talking about the amazing runners in the London Marathon today, I have to say I have such admiration for the dedication and effort it takes to be involved, it's amazing how many people will "pay forward" their love and energy to raise so much for charity.

If you've never come across the concept, I'd urge you to seek out the film of the same name (Pay it Forwards).

Another conversation I became involved in talked about being a go-giver...which takes the old adage of the business "go-getter" and turns it on its head, suggesting that in business and in life you need to become a "go-giver". Giving with a servant's heart (giving without expectation of return) is something I do strongly believe myself.

All this along with the suggestion from a friend to write about, "how people do their bit for good causes".

So the topic for today is clear..."Will you do something amazing today?"

I have already mentioned "starting a ripple". It's amazing just how one small act of kindness; acting with a servant's heart, can lead to miraculous effects on your loved ones, your community, your country and even the world.

If everyone did just one small thing, imagine what the effect might be?

Take the "pay it forward" equation...pay forward three good deeds to three people, without expectation of return, in turn they pay forward three good deeds to 3 people, on and on it goes.... (Yes, I did do the maths and it turns into a very big number)...Very soon before you know it, the act of paying it forwards has grown into a massive wave from the smallest ripple...

Why not start right now?

Creating that ripple right now YOU could very quickly encompass the whole world! How's that for global expansion?

Exciting prospect?

It could be the smallest thing that YOU pay forward RIGHT NOW, TODAY, a smile and a hug, your time, your advice, a gift...That turns into something huge! And what a priceless gift to give to those that really need it!

And you know what?

When YOU "pay it forwards" you have to be in a place of abundance, for in order to give it away YOU have to have it in the first place!

Think about that for a moment...YOU have to have it, in order to give it away!

So the act of giving reminds us how very blessed and abundant we are!

It's amazing what a small act of kindness can achieve, in giving something amazing occurs, not only do we make a difference to another...we receive!

For it is in giving that we receive
~ St. Francis of Assisi

Exercise: Do something amazing today.

So today, I urge you to do something amazing, act with a servant's heart, pay it forwards, bless another with a random act of kindness...start a ripple...

Note down your experience.

10

What story will you create today?

To be a person is to have a story to tell.
~ Isak Dinesen

Today sees most of the children returning to school after half-term break. From the numerous internet posts I've read this morning, maybe parents are a little keener to get back to "normal" and school runs than their offspring, but it did make me think about today's chapter!

Do you remember that first day back to school after the holidays?

I recall as a primary-school child, writing in my diary at school, capturing all of the events and activities I'd experienced during the school break. It was a story that revelled in those newly built memories, written with fondness, and happiness at creating in my mind's eye the words and pictures that represented every juicy detail of my holiday fun.

It made me realise that often as adults we don't always take the time to really savour our experiences, to tell our story, to create a keepsake of our fond memories. Every day we start afresh with a blank page on which to make our mark, to build new memories, to create the story and book of our life.

When Stories nestle in the body, soul comes forth.
~ Deena Metzger

The finished product of what you write for today is completely your choice. How you choose to make your mark upon the world today is up to you. In each unfolding chapter you shape the part you play, your role and your experiences.

Exercise: What story will you create today?

So I invite you to look at today as a blank page, a fresh crispy clear start on which to make your mark.

What role will you choose for yourself today?
Are you leading lady/ handsome hero?
Who shares your story?
Are you joyful and abundant?
What colour expresses the mood of your day?
If you were painting a picture of today, what would you include in the illustration?
Capture your storyline for today:

And at the end of the day, how will you savour and appreciate today's experiences and gifts?

Life itself is the most wonderful fairytale of all.
~ Hans Christian Andersen

11

If you want it...You just have to believe!

I had the pleasure of rediscovering a beautiful song "Believe" by Lenny Kravitz recently. It was thanks to my amazing friend Lisa Gates, she said it was my song, the song that she associated with me...It wasn't until I listened to it again, for the first time in years, that I really heard the words! I was very humbled to realise that Lisa felt this summed up how I portrayed myself and my work... but truly blessed and grateful to be considered in this way.

It did urge me to write today's chapter...About what is possible if only we believe...If we are free to truly be ourselves, and live a joyful and loving life!

Miracles can occur if only we can believe that they can. It's a state of mind...our choice...

On listening to the song again a few things stood out. Firstly, for me I was reminded that we have everything we could possibly imagine, if we just believe in ourselves, we are free to be ourselves and express ourselves just as we are!

And secondly, we can sometimes just get caught up in life, It reminded me that we can so easily get caught up in our stories...we can so easily take life way too seriously, when in truth it's a game, we can play, we can believe, we can live in total wonderment.

I remember: if I take myself back to my corporate career, sitting in a particular meeting one Monday morning, where the discussion about the next product promotion had the tone of a "life or death" situation...I recall it now just as if I were there...a moment of clarity...one of those "I just woke up" moments and realised "What is this all about? What am I doing here?" ...My colleagues in the meeting were so caught up in the story; they acted out the seriousness of the topic...I felt the odd one out...I do remember thinking, why are we taking something such as a product promotion quite so seriously? Life is for living, for being joyful...there are serious times in life, of course...but truly was this one of them?...

I wonder how much more successful said product promotion may have been, if it had just been approached with joy instead.

Exercise: If you want it you just have to believe

So I urge you today to ask yourself these questions:

Where are you getting caught up in the (or someone else's) "Story"?

What do you stand for, what really matters?

What does being FREE mean to you?

What could you achieve if only you could believe?

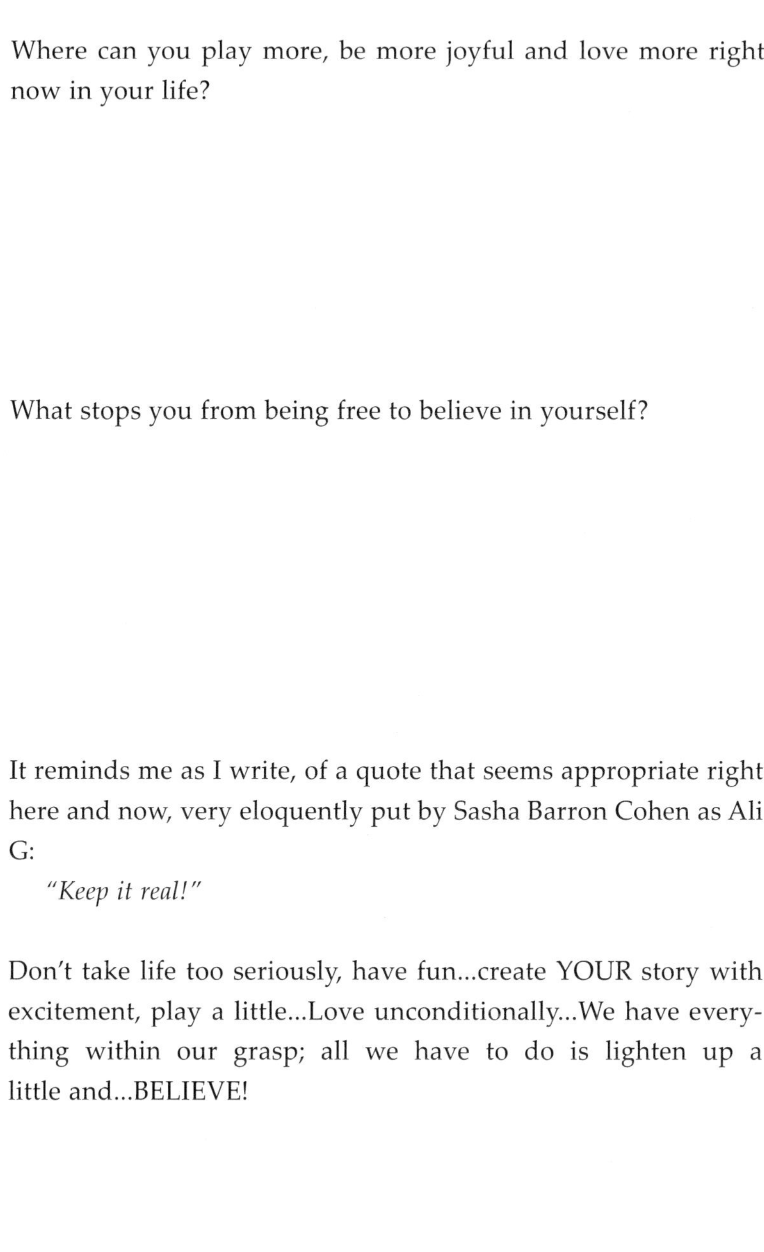

Where can you play more, be more joyful and love more right now in your life?

What stops you from being free to believe in yourself?

It reminds me as I write, of a quote that seems appropriate right here and now, very eloquently put by Sasha Barron Cohen as Ali G:

"Keep it real!"

Don't take life too seriously, have fun...create YOUR story with excitement, play a little...Love unconditionally...We have everything within our grasp; all we have to do is lighten up a little and...BELIEVE!

12

Nothing is ever wasted if it's recycled!

Have you ever had a Job you hated?

Maybe you're in that situation right now?

It can be so frustrating being "stuck" in a miserable job.

(Just Over Broke, too much month left at the end of the money)

But were you, or are you truly "stuck"?

Life flows in cycles, you can flow with it or against it. Everything we do has meaning, sometimes we just have to look a little deeper to understand exactly what that is.

Consider this...Think of a time when you were in a job, doing work that you thought was unfulfilling, without meaning, work that didn't exactly make your heart sing and spirit soar...Thought of one?

Now with this particular work in mind, consider the following...

(If it helps, make a list, write it down)

What skills and knowledge did you need to carry out the work?

What did it teach you?

What did you learn about yourself?

What aspects of the work really encouraged you to grow?

What aspects did you enjoy?

What clues did it give you as to your true purpose?

Even if it taught you that it wasn't the work you were born to do, that "it" wasn't your purpose...It did give you that gift!

As we journey through life we accumulate knowledge and skills, we learn as we go, we're always a work in progress. I can think of several times in my life when I found myself in work that wasn't fulfilling, or obviously meaningful...However, despite that, in hindsight if I really consider every aspect of those jobs, whilst they weren't necessarily my "purpose", they were preparing me with the necessary skills, knowledge and attributes for the vocation I now follow. I have learnt a lot, those times have helped to form the person I have become and am still becoming!

Now think about the very worst job you ever had...

What skills and knowledge do you recycle today from that time?

What did you learn from that time that could be recycled now today, that you're currently not using?

When I consider the work that has gone before, there are many skills and pieces of knowledge that I recycle and use in my work today.

And if you're reading this and thinking, "But I hate my job now!", consider...

What learning opportunities is it providing you with that you're not embracing?

What would you need to do, be or have to make you feel more "on purpose"?

If you could change your work tomorrow, knowing that with your accumulated knowledge and skills, you couldn't fail...

What would you do?

Every day on this journey is the chance to learn and apply what we've already learnt and experienced. What I've observed is that we naturally tend to recycle from those jobs and work we've loved...it's the times that we feel have been a "waste" that we dismiss, when in fact this is where some of the greatest "nuggets" of learning and self-development can be gained!

Nothing is ever wasted if it's recycled!

Exercise: Nothing's wasted if it's recycled

What could YOU be recycling today?

13

Carpe Diem

Carpe diem ***Latin['kɑːpɪ 'diːɛm]*** enjoy the pleasures of the moment, without concern for the future [literally: seize the day!]

I was considering what to write about today. Then it occurred to me...over the past few months I've been blessed to work with many amazing people in many different workshops. What has become apparent to me is that, in these workshops I have witnessed so many participants "seizing the day", throwing themselves into the learning opportunity with passion and wild abandon!

It's a true joy to work with these people over a period of months, seeing their growth, sharing their journey. They squeeze every last drop from the opportunity to develop themselves, and they have fun!

But there are those; a small minority, who despite having made a conscious choice to attend, aren't able to "let go" and fully engage. Of course we're all on our own personal journey and only the individual themselves can make the choice to grow or stay stuck. But it did make me consider what's going on there? Why do some people just relish the change and some people push it away when they so clearly crave to change themselves, their situation or their environment?

The main difference I have noticed is where the individuals feel "responsibility" lies. Those who have come to believe that they are responsible for steering their own lives, despite their surroundings and situations, really move forward at a rate of knots, they appear limitless and create and manifest their greatest dreams.

However, those who place the responsibility outside of themselves, blaming others, their environment, their situation, everything and everyone, not considering themselves, seem to stay stuck, going round in continuous circles of frustration, disappointment and limits, no matter what tools and gifts of shared knowledge is imparted.

But what's the root cause?

Why do some people take responsibility and some people give away responsibility?

LOVE or FEAR

If you consider for a moment, all emotions, the full range of emotional responses. When it comes down to it, there really are just two base emotions, from which all other emotions arise, LOVE and FEAR, every emotional response can be categorised as either emanating from LOVE or FEAR. Try it out...think of an emotion now...which does it emanate from, LOVE or FEAR ?

Those that love themselves enough and love those around them...choose to act in accordance with the heart, their empowering beliefs...they consciously choose the ability to determine their response...and they choose LOVE.

Those that FEAR, choose to act in accordance with their limiting beliefs they don't recognise their ability to actively choose their response and remain stuck in FEAR (False Evidence Appearing Real)...Waiting or allowing a situation or another person to choose for them.

But there is a question that can unlock this limitation...

If you should ever find yourself stuck or fearful of "seizing the day" and diving right in ask yourself: "What would LOVE do?"

"Your time is limited, so don't waste it living someone else's life. Don't be trapped by dogma – which is living with the results of other people's thinking. Don't let the noise of other's opinions drown out your own inner voice. And most important, have the courage to

follow your heart and intuition. They somehow already know what you truly want to become. Everything else is secondary."
~Steve Jobs
Carpe diem ~Seize the day

Exercise: Carpe diem

Today I urge you to capture every opportunity that you've seized.

What have you experienced and learnt as a result?

14

Do you have a spring in your step?

Its the first day of spring as I write today – it made me consider this question:

Do you have a spring in your step?

I've noticed the morning birdsong getting earlier over the past couple of weeks, the garden is starting to wake up from its winter slumber and the sun has certainly been making an appearance the past few days.

I love the springtime, for me it means new beginnings, new growth, freshness and expectation of what lies ahead! It's also time to go outside, get some fresh air having been cooped up all winter!

Traditionally, this time of year is a powerful time to focus on courage, action, passion, overcoming obstacles, new business ventures, for physical strength and independence. In everyday life the coming of spring is the time to throw out the old to make way for the new – hence the term "spring cleaning". It's a time to consider what you can let go of...what you no longer need, what slows you down, saps your energy and no longer serves you. Let it go in order to make way for the new.

What can you "spring clean" in your life?

Questions to consider:

What will I let go of today?

What one limiting thought will I eliminate today?

What old "Things" can I donate, recycle or throw away?

What do I want to invite into my life today?

What one empowering thought will I adopt today?
What will I manifest in my life today?
Putting a spring in your step.

Exercise: Put a spring in your step

If you're not quite bouncing like Tigger today, don't worry here's my top tips to getting in tune with the energy of spring!

Put a spring in your step:

Clear out the clutter, de clutter your space, your home, your office, your wardrobe.

Get out into nature, go to the park, take a walk, sit by a river or stream.

Clear the garden; sweep the path, plant something new.

Write down every aspect of your life you'd like to let go of, then burn it.

Create your vision board, (you can contact me for more details of how to do this!)

Listen to uplifting music

Sing out loud

Dance

Play

Laugh

...the list is endless...Please feel free to add your own ideas!

15

Expect a Miracle

BELIEVE IN YOUR HEART

Believe in your heart that something wonderful is about to happen. Love your life. Believe in your own powers, and your own potential, and in your own innate goodness. Wake every morning with the awe of just being alive. Discover each day the magnificent, awesome beauty in the world. Explore and embrace life in yourself and in everyone you see each day. Reach within to find your own specialness. Amaze yourself and rouse those around you to the potential of each new day. Don't be afraid to admit that you are less than perfect; this is the essence of your humanity. Let those who love you help you. Trust enough to be able to take. Look with hope to the horizon of today, for today is all we truly have. Live this day well. Let a little sun out as well as in. Create your own rainbows. Be open to all your possibilities; all possibilities and Miracles. Always believe in Miracles.

~ Author Unknown

Do you believe in miracles?

Did you wake this morning and expect miracles to occur, or did you simply expect a day like any other?

What counts as a miracle in your life?

I woke this morning with an overwhelming feeling of excitement; I couldn't name the reason for it, just a wonderful optimistic start to the day. Miracles can be the most simple of occurrences though don't you think? How much do we take for granted? As I look back at my day small miracles have followed me all day long...I woke this morning, still breathing, healthy and strong, with the love of my life next to me...I had all I needed to keep me warm, fed and clothed; I had hot and plentiful water for my bath...I was blessed to do the work I love this morning, before heading off to meet my beautiful daughter from college, she had arranged for us to have lunch at The George in Stamford as well as meeting a dear friend for coffee whom I hadn't seen for a long time.

When we arrived despite a busy town centre a parking place was available just where and when we needed it…And so my day went on. Now you could say there's not really very much miraculous about my day...but all the way along I have been blessed with little miracles.

If little miracles can come my way, then so can big ones too...All it takes is gratitude and belief that all is possible. We make our own miracles every day...we maybe just forget to notice them.

RECIPE FOR A MIRACLE

- 1 cup Tension
- 2 cups Stress
- 1 teaspoon of Guilt
- 2 heaping cups of Limited Time
- 3/4 tablespoon of Urgency
- A dash of "No Other Choice"
- 3 heaping cups of Faith

Fold ingredients gently into a bowl. Mix vigorously and add a few tears. You'll sweat a little as you knead the dough. Pack it firmly between your hopes and dreams and form into a perfect little ball. Sprinkle it with a little faith, rolling the ball in the flour until fully covered. Place it under a veil of belief and allow it to rise. Put it in an oven that has been pre-set at the perfect temperature for the heat of trials and tribulations. Allow it to brown under the warmth of love. Remove after due season and allow to cool in the confidence of promise. Garnish with your praises.

Arrange neatly on a platter of thankfulness and serve to friends, families and, oh yes, strangers...invite them too! Pass on the recipe to all who request it and let them know that with this recipe, they have the makings of a miracle! ~ Author Unknown

Exercise: Believe in miracles

Today I urge you to capture every little miracle that you're grateful for.

16

Nam-myoho-renge-kyo

Just last Saturday myself and my partner, Jon, found ourselves in one of our favourite bookshops. Browsing bookshops is personally one of my favourite pastimes, I find the energy of all that knowledge and adventure captured in the written word and recorded on the page for all time, an inspiration.

Both Jon and I have heaps of interesting books, and our thirst for knowledge and learning means that we have a shared love of reading.

As is usual for me I browsed the psychology, self-help and philosophy sections before moving on to the mind, body and spirit section. Two synchronistic moments occurred...earlier that day I had been scanning through the local paper to see an advert for a "Life club" which caught my eye, I thought briefly, that's an interesting concept...As I moved ahead of Jon to the next section in the bookshop, he held up a brightly coloured book "The Life Book"...he flicked through it and said, "hold onto this one, I like the look of it!"....As I opened it up to have a little flick through it myself...what did I see?...you guessed it, it was written by the same woman (Nina Grunfeld) who was the founder of "Life clubs"!...well we just had to have that book, after all how much clearer could the universe be in spelling it out that we should???

Next as I walked towards the mind, body and spirit section, there right in front of me was "Cosmic energy" by Anne Jirsch, now I had recently struck up conversation with Anne on Twitter...Having no idea at that point that she was an author or that we shared such a similar view on cosmic energy...so you guessed it that was my purchase of the day...I did also see a book by another famous author I've briefly Twittered with too, but that one will wait until my next visit I think!

On getting back home, cup of tea in hand, Jon was already engrossed in his book , and I opened up "Cosmic energy"...I have to say I couldn't put Anne's book down, some of the material is very similar to the topics that I teach myself, some of the exercises are new to me and some parts of the book have brought back to me things I had long since forgotten...Which leads me onto...

Nam-myoho-renge-kyo....

Loosely translated it means:
Nam - Devotion to the mystic law
Myoho - The mystic law - the law of life
Renge-Of the lotus -the lotus blossom representing Karma
Kyo- Sutra- the voice itself - the teaching of Buddha

The phrase NAM-MYOHO-RENGE-KYO is taken from one of greatest teachings of the first recorded Buddha. This teaching, called the Lotus Sutra, says that all living beings, regardless of gender or intelligence (that means everyone – including you and me!), have the potential to attain Buddhahood. In the Lotus Sutra, Shakyamuni Buddha teaches that inside each one of us is a universal truth known as the Buddha nature. Basing our lives on this Buddha nature enables us to enjoy absolute happiness and to act with endless compassion. This state of happiness is called enlightenment. It's simply waking up to the true nature of life, realising that all things are connected, and that there is such a close relationship between each and every one of us and our surroundings that when we change ourselves, we change the world.

Imagine that for a moment...When we change ourselves, we change the World!

I must thank Anne for helping me to remember to chant Nam-myoho-renge-kyo, why not give it a try yourself? Imagine for a moment the positive effect of everyone connecting with that inner knowing of total compassion, peace and connectedness...just imagine what transformation can occur by the ripple effect of each one of us making a small and positive change today...in turn how that would change our world!

So I urge you today to join me in making a positive change!

Exercise: Practicing Nam-myoho-renge-kyo

Over the next week, capture what happens when you chant Nam-myoho-renge-kyo morning, noon and night.

What magic will enter your life and therefore mine too!

17

Don't be a salmon

This afternoon I was reminded of a lovely lady I once worked with whilst I was still back in my corporate career, working as an area manager in a well-known high street bank.

This inspiring lady came to mind as a result of a rather frustrating technical hitch between myself and my computer!

(Taking my own advice I turned my frustration into fascination, hence I stopped what I was doing and wrote this chapter instead!)

I recall a similarly frustrating day whilst still working for the bank, luckily for me, that particular day I arrived for an afternoon meeting with this calm and wonderful woman. She was a wise and gentle woman, I seem to remember she was in the Salvation Army outside of her "Day job" I know she gave many hours of her time to help people less fortunate than herself. She was thoughtful, loving and kind; I really enjoyed working alongside her (despite her particular job being an auditing type role!)

Anyway, It must have been quite obvious that I had had a very frustrating morning, but she simply smiled and put the kettle on!

Whilst she made the tea I noticed a black and white photocopy pinned to her notice board. It was a picture of a salmon, with the phrase "Don't be a salmon" typed above it.

A couple of minutes later, she handed me my very welcome cup of tea, thanking her, I enquired; now intrigued, what the picture and phrase meant.

She explained that in life we can either go with the flow or against it...If we flow with life, then it's a beautiful journey, calm, supported, and in simple terms it just moves along more easily.

However, if we choose to swim against the flow, its hard work, tiring, frustrating, limiting and we use up so much energy just trying to keep up the fight against the current, we simply don't get to enjoy the journey.

I paused to think about this...She then went on to say (which I didn't realise at the time) that the salmon risks life and fin (excuse the pun) to swim upstream to spawn its eggs, it battles against the flow, it's a hard and tiring journey...eventually the salmon, exhausted from its journey, reaches the end of its swim and spawns its eggs...the salmon will then usually die within the next seven days.

Whilst this is the ultimate sacrifice to reproduce...The photocopied piece of paper of course then made perfect sense to me...It was a reminder...

"Don't be a salmon!" ...don't spend your life and your journey, constantly swimming against the flow of life...to then come to the end and to have struggled throughout and not savoured the beautiful scenery along the way!

So, this afternoon, when my computer hitch made me feel frustrated and as though I was efforting and getting nowhere...I remembered the salmon!

I immediately stopped what I was doing, made a cup of tea, took some deep breaths and got back into the flow!

Re-energised...back in the flow and inspired to share this chapter with you!

Exercise: Don't be a salmon

So, I urge you today to consider:

Where are you efforting , but simply treading water?

Where are you swimming against the tide?

What would you need to change for you to get back into the flow?

What action can you take right now, that will allow flow into your life and work?

Let go and let flow!

18

Why be ordinary when you can be extraordinary?

I have my other half Jon to thank for today's chapter!

He showed me an amazing man doing ordinary work in an extraordinary way, thus transforming the mundane into the magnificent! In a You Tube video he shared with me the awe inspiring Billy Clean...Who must be the happiest street sweeper I've ever seen!

The video shows the street cleaner, dancing in a Michael Jackson style as he cleans the streets and litter-picks!

Imagine putting that amount of love and joy into your work every day!

It doesn't matter what your vocation happens to be, you can choose to be ordinary or as in Billy Clean's case extraordinary!

If a man is called to be a street sweeper, he should sweep streets even as Michelangelo painted or Beethoven composed music or Shakespeare wrote poetry. He should sweep streets so well that all the hosts of heaven and earth will pause to say, 'Here lived a great street sweeper who did his job well.'"

What makes the difference?

It's all about attitude! You choose every morning if you will face the day with positivity or negativity.

In Billy Clean's case, quite obviously he chooses to carry out his work positively, bringing joy not only to himself, but to everyone he meets.

The streets he sweeps have become his stage, he has chosen a starring role, and he is really sharing his love of life with everyone who should pass down his street. Bringing a little more happiness to those he serves.

Act as if what you do makes a difference. It does
~ William James

Never doubt your influence on the world around you.

We are all inextricably linked and interwoven with each other and everything that exists.

Never doubt your ability to make a difference...for every action there is a reaction...cause and effect...

Exercise: Why be ordinary when you can be extraordinary?

So no matter what your vocation, I urge you to consider:
How can you carry out your work more joyfully today?

How can you be extraordinary today?

How can you change the mundane into the magnificent today?

Be bold, be unique, and be extraordinary in all you do today...

19

Rain and shifting tides

Following on from unseasonably hot weather for May, June began with a cold and very wet start yesterday. I found myself wondering how long it would be before we would see "summer" once more. Around me everyone seemed to be unhappy about the dull and dreary weather, it really was noticeable that the weather change had affected people's mood. In truth of course it wasn't the weather, just their reaction to it!

As I looked out of the window yesterday afternoon, the rain was pouring down, I too was wishing for sun. It was then it struck me, the garden had come to life, everything was seemingly growing right in front of my eyes. It was at that moment that it occurred to me, without the rain the growth wouldn't happen.

"Life is like a rainbow. You need both the sun and the rain to make its colours appear."

In my teaching as a therapist, water represents emotion. As humans we're predominately made up of water...therefore we're also pretty emotional beings.

It occurred to me that we not only need the water to survive physically, but emotionally and spiritually too. By experiencing love and fear and all of the emotions in between, just like the rain follows the sun and the sun follows the rain...growth comes from the full range of experience. If we did not have both sun and rain, the garden wouldn't grow and bloom.

Are we not then the same?

Do we need the shifting tides in order to grow?

If we consider the shifting tides for just a moment...Tides are created because the earth and the moon are attracted to each other, just like magnets are attracted to each other. The moon tries to pull at anything on the earth to bring it closer. But, the earth is able to hold onto everything except the water. Since the water is always moving, (In flow) the earth cannot hold onto it, and the moon is able to pull at it. Each day, there are two high tides and two low tides. The ocean is constantly moving from high tide to low tide, and then back to high tide. It seems that in nature we can see the ebb and flow all around us...

Yet we surely are only experiencing and replicating the same within ourselves?

The ebb and flow that provide us the opportunity to grow.

Exercise: Rain and shifting tides

Today I urge you to recognise the gifts of both the sun and the rain. Allow the ebb and flow of the shifting tides within your life, understand that it is simply the natural cycle of life.

Welcome the opportunity to grow...then just let yourself blossom!

"Anyone who says only sunshine brings happiness has never danced in the rain"

20

Love your shoes

When writing I always ask for guidance about what to write, what will be of most use to you the reader? This guidance comes in many forms, sometimes a thought that comes to mind, a symbol or sign...for this entry the guidance has come in the form of a pair of shoes!

Recently my gorgeous partner, Jon, bought me some new sandals for the summer. They're very pretty, with flower shapes running through the front, in a gold colour...so pleased have I been with them I've worn them often over the past couple of weeks. I thought I'd really write today!

It was just now as I took them off, I noticed that on the inside there's gold lettering...it reads "Love your shoes"...I couldn't believe I hadn't noticed this detail. I sat for a moment wondering what on Earth "Love your shoes" had to do with this chapter.

Then, like a bolt of lightning it came to me...of course!

> *Standing in someone else's shoes for a second, it suddenly dawns on you.*
> *~ Mel Gibson*

Your feet and your shoes carry you through life. Shoes in this case are a metaphor for your life journey. Actors such as Mel Gibson above get the opportunity to "try on" many pairs of shoes in their career; they step into the life and journey of the characters they portray. Of course it's not really like living the life of their characters, but it does make you think.

Wherever your shoes are headed right now, with you wearing them you are making a choice, you are starting with a single step...what direction are you going in?

Maybe you're not happy with your lot...Imagine this if you were to try on someone else's shoes, who would you choose? And more importantly why?

Now for a moment think of someone less fortunate than yourself...really try to imagine what it might be like to walk in their shoes for a day?

Are your shoes feeling a little more comfy right now?

I found this quote from Billy Bob Thornton which I found to be very thought provoking...

When people wear shoes that don't fit them, it says something about their soul.
~Billy Bob Thornton

When we try to squeeze into shoes that don't fit us, it hurts, it's painful, and it takes all of our focus and energy just noticing how very uncomfortable it feels.

It's just the same in our life!

When we try to "fit" into a role, relationship, job, environment, or way of being that isn't truly us, our spirit feels hurt, in pain, our focus and energy becomes tunnelled into noticing just how very uncomfortable it feels.

Exercise: Love your shoes

So today I urge you to consider...
How much do you love your shoes?

If you could change them for something more fitting and comfortable what would they look and feel like?

And just for fun...
If you were a pair of shoes...what would they be?

What does that tell you about your soul's longing?

21

Speak your truth

I caught a film halfway through last night, I can't actually recall the title of the film, but what did stick with me was a quote from the scene I saw...it went something like this:

"Why just follow someone else's thoughts? There'd be no point in thinking yourself!"

Now there's something to consider...We are given the gift of our own thoughts, but very often we become governed by other's thoughts, instead of our own?

Now I'm not saying we should never agree with the thoughts of another, not at all...But sometimes we can become stuck, following someone else's route map, putting our own to one side. Not trusting our own thoughts and more importantly our own inner guidance.

How many times have you bitten your tongue, held back from expressing your own truth?

Why is that?

I understand there may be many reasons to not speak up or speak out, but is your truth any less true than the next person?

Your truth is simply your point of reference, your perspective, your vantage point in the world from which you view life through your eyes. It's not cast in stone, it's not static but fluid and developing as you learn and grow.

By speaking our truth we may not always be popular, but it is by expressing our truth we give ourselves and others the opportunity to grow. When you speak your truth you are sharing your view of the World, its unique to you...the world through your eyes...Just as when another speaks their truth, you are being gifted a small window through which to view the world as they see it.

By sharing in this way, we give each other the opportunity to consider new ways of seeing, new ways of being and a whole new world opens up to be explored. If you always bite your tongue, hold back, hold your thoughts, then you're denying the development of yourself and the rest of the world!

You may not agree with my writing, and you know what?

That's brilliant!...Without different views to see, different scenery to enjoy, life would be stagnant and a little boring.

If you have a strong urge to speak your truth today, I urge you to go for it!

Speak from the heart, with love and compassion, with respect and willingness to grow and learn. That's when the magic begins, ideas and thoughts meld, and develop...remember the saying "Two heads are better than one" this is a perfect example of how speaking one's truth can be the work of an alchemist, creating nuggets of gold from a tiny seed of an idea or thought, creating something so abundant the whole evolution of the world actually depends on it!

Imagine this...it's not so long ago people believed the Earth to be flat…it's true, the great scholars truly believed with all their heart that the Earth was flat.

Imagine then how it was for the first person who spoke their truth and said that the Earth was in fact round?

Imagine if they had bitten their tongue, held their peace, not spoken their truth?

Now I'm sure they were perhaps a little nervous before they expressed their truth, maybe they fought an internal conflict with all they had previously been conditioned to believe.

But they stood strong and spoke their truth, despite any fear of ridicule or rejection...They just went ahead and said it anyway! It was as a result of their courage to speak from the heart, to share their view (albeit a new round one) of the world, that I'm sure debates and discussions ensued...but the gift was the courage to speak, allowing the outcome of new knowledge and new growth for the whole world.

Exercise: Speak your truth

So I urge you today.....

Speak your truth, with love and respect; please share the gift of how the World looks to you, because I can't see through your eyes.

Capture the truths you shared today.

22

Bend with the breeze

It's been an interesting couple of weeks.

My diary was perfectly planned; workshops and social activities booked into the diary, the month of June looked full and abundant as I looked at my schedule.

Work schedules were healthy and in balance, financial forecasts for the month's income looked good. I even had time for social events planned with Jon, my friends and family. What a perfectly planned June I had ahead!

And then it happened...Everything started to shift... Workshops rescheduled, clients having to cancel last minute, Jon getting a bad cold, meaning we had to cancel prior arrangements. Now I could have got frustrated, down hearted, negative...But I didn't, I just stopped!

I recognised I was being given an opportunity....

How would I respond?

Would I panic?

Would I use the opportunity wisely?

Would I get busy doing busy work, without stopping to consider why I had this time being gifted to me?

I simply stopped, took a deep breath, lit some candles, some incense, cleared my working space of any stagnant energy with Reiki and sound, then asked and waited for guidance.

I felt perfectly calm, perfectly centred and in total balance.

For a long time now I have been thinking about writing...working on not one but four book ideas.

What was holding me back?

Now I could make every excuse under the sun as to why...but in truth, I realised that there must be some fear preventing me from simply getting on with it. The more I tried the less I could write...until now...Now I had been given all the time, resources, space and opportunity to write. Nothing else demanding my time, not even the housework!

So I began...and I allowed, but didn't push.

As ideas and thoughts came to me, or as I asked for guidance on what to write next, the words just flowed...and when they didn't I stopped once more.

I didn't try to force it. I simply bent with the breeze, moved with the flow, and didn't think or worry about anything but the moment of writing as it came.

I can hear you saying...but there're bills to pay, school runs to do...I couldn't be so indulgent. Well I say, why not?

Why not stop and observe what you're doing, or not doing?

It reminds me of a quote I read "When life gives you lemons, make lemonade!"

So, yes, I could have gone into panic mode, I could have worried myself about lack, I could have made excuses not to write, labelling it as time wasting, indulgent, or that it'll never be good enough.

But I didn't, I took the opportunity to bend with the breeze, to flow with the opportunity...to do something I am truly passionate about...which is to share with you through my writing!

Exercise: Bend with the breeze

So next time your plans go astray...ask yourself:
Why is it?

What's the opportunity I'm being given?

And what will I do with it?

23

If not now, when?

How time flies by, someone asked me in conversation the other day how old my daughter is...she's 19...it occurred to me how very quickly the time has passed.

In the blink of an eye, that cute little toddler covered in chocolate has transformed into a beautiful young woman. How did that happen? How fast the years have flown!

Do you recall being a small child at infant or primary school?

Is it just me, or were the days much longer then? Was it a trick of the mind that a week seemed a lifetime, and a year an eternity?

Then comes the teenage years, where Sundays were BORING, and getting up before lunchtime was a waste of a good sleep, funny though however that time spent on revision seemed endless and torturous.

Next came BIG plans, the world was my oyster...I had all the time in the world, opportunities abounded...all the time in the world to make my mark.

How then did time speed up? How did it change from week-long eternities of me as a 5-year-old child to "Where did those years go?"

There are whole years for which I hope I'll never be cross-examined, for I could not give an alibi
~ Mignon McLaughlin

I write at the end of each of my blog postings "Make every moment count" and I truly mean that. Because time, this time around, is precious.

Which reminds me...have you seen the film "The Bucket List"

it's a great film. It's a story of corporate billionaire Edward Cole and working-class mechanic Carter Chambers who have nothing in common except for their terminal illnesses.

While sharing a hospital room together, they decide to leave it and do all the things they have ever wanted to do before they die according to their "Bucket List". In the process, both of them heal each other, become unlikely friends, and ultimately find the joy in life.

Whilst this heartwarming film is a fictional story, isn't it so often true, that we wait until we get an almighty wakeup call before we start living. In most cases thankfully it's not as a result of serious illness, but all too often we put off our dreams...

Until we've finished school
Until we've finished college/university
Until we've got a better job/more money
Until we settle down/get married
Until we've had a family/ kids are at school/ kids are off hand
Until we have more time...

Time is the coin of your life. It is the only coin you have, and only you can determine how it will be spent. Be careful lest you let other people spend it for you.
~ Carl Sandburg

Don't wait until life kicks you in the backside, make the moment count now!

Exercise: If not now, when?

So today I urge you to consider:

What dreams have you put on the backburner?

What joy are you delaying?

What's really stopping you?

What would you write on your "Bucket List"?

And what do you want to have achieved in this life before it's over?

Begin it! Begin it now!
If not now, when?
What are you waiting for?
Make every moment count.

24

Ignite the spirit

Today I was thinking about the spirit light within. No matter what is going on around us, difficult situations, challenging relationships, the spark of our spirit is always intact. It cannot be extinguished. Even in death the spirit light continues, it is our essence, carried throughout lifetimes, in between lifetimes and beyond. Science tells us that we are made up of energy, it also tells us that energy cannot be destroyed only changed in form.

The spirit light within us is the very core of us, it's the part of us that unifies us with everyone and every other thing. At the very spark of us, we're all the same – all of the same flame.

So even when our outer physical self may seem trapped and restricted, in truth we are always free, as you may recall I've written before.

I find it inspiring to consider this spark!

inspire [ɪn'spaɪə] *vb*
To guide or arouse by divine influence or inspiration
To breathe life into

This spark is there within us no matter who or where you are, it is alive and present.

If we tap into our spark, our light, we can ignite our spirit and in doing so we also have the opportunity to ignite the light within others.

Thousands of candles can be lit from a single candle, and the life of the candle will not be shortened. Happiness never decreases by being shared. ~ Buddha

Exercise: Visulisation on Igniting the spark

Imagine that spark within you now, picture it in your mind's eye.

Is it a tiny spark?

A glowing ember?

A flickering flame?

A roaring fire of energy?

And if it's not a beautiful flame, consider:

What would you need to feel, to be in order to visualise your spark into a flame?

Keep your focus on igniting your spirit. Imagine in your mind's eye that spark growing brighter and brighter...

Its becoming a beautiful flame of light...glowing brighter and brighter...see it expanding now...bigger and bigger, until every cell of your body is light and bright!

Now, expand that light out, until it's outside of yourself, out further into the room, the space, the environment you're in...keep on expanding it, further and further, out into the street, the garden, the park, fields, the whole neighbourhood, the country, the world, as far as you can imagine.

Now do you realise just how limitless you are?

How magnificent and miraculous you are?

Your spark is the individual essence of you and your spirit, but it is also the essence that connects each and every one of us, in fact every living thing.

So, going back to where we started. Now you realise that you can ignite your spirit, more than that, you can ignite the spirit in others too. You expanded you light beyond the confines of yourself...way beyond! You are never trapped or limited never truly stuck.

Ignite your spirit and you can light up the world!

25

Great weather for ducks!

As I popped to the post office earlier today, I noticed a single duck sitting by the roadside. It was a mallard I believe with beautiful green chest feathers.

By now you'll probably realise that when such things are brought into my awareness it's generally for a reason!

So true to form, once I returned home I looked up the symbolism of duck as a totem. I already knew the heart centred symbolism of the beautiful green coloured feathers.

Duck:

Emotional Comfort and Protection.

Ducks are associated with the element of water.

They are good deep water swimmers and also are content to glide on top of a body of water.

As a totem the duck teaches getting in touch with your deepest emotions in order to get to a calmer state.

Ducks are family oriented and enjoy companionship. If a duck visits it could mean it is time to return to your roots and spend some time with your clan.

Eckhart Tolle, best-selling author of A New Earth *often tells a story about how ducks do not hold grudges. They will ruffle their feathers and get in a snit with another duck over differences but within minutes later the argument is forgotten and the duck is calm and serene on the lake. Duck medicine teaches us not to hold on to our past troubles and to live in the moment.*

Ducks are also connected to feminine energies, the astral plane and emotions through their connection with water.

Ducks remind us to drink deeply from the waters of life.

Find comfort in your element and with those of like mind and spirit. Ducks teach you how to manoeuvre through the waters of life with grace and comfort.

Psychologist and therapists often have Ducks as a totem, assisting them to help others move through emotional tangles.

How interesting that Duck should make his presence known, whilst I'm considering what to write for you today!

When doubt creeps in and we re-run old programmes, signs such as duck pop up to remind us to enjoy life in the moment, don't live life NOW by life back then. For that moment no longer exists and this moment is where life is happening!

Life is what happens while you are busy making other plans.
~ John Lennon

No matter what's going on in your life right now, it is a manifestation of your thoughts and feelings of the past, so if you want something different, you need to start thinking and feeling in this moment, not re-running the old thoughts and feelings of the past.

Duck reminds us to honour our deepest feelings and emotions, to drink in life! He teaches us to follow our feminine energy to nurture and to create. To hold companionship, family and community in the heart of us. As that's what's important and sustains us, just as the water element that he represents.

Duck is a great reminder to let go of petty squabbles, ride above the waves, and enjoy the flow. He also tells us to surround ourselves with those of a like mind that we may support one another as we learn and grow.

I particularly like the line that says *"Ducks teach you how to manoeuvre through the waters of life with grace and comfort."*

So no matter what your situation, right now, no matter what you may be manoeuvring around in your life, know that you have comfort and that you can act with grace.

grace

n.

A disposition to be generous or helpful; goodwill.

Divine love and protection bestowed freely on people.

The state of being protected.

You see the signs are always there if we just take time to notice them!

Nice weather for Ducks don't you think?

Exercise: Noticing the signs

Today I urge you to make a note of any signs that appear to you.

What do they mean to you?

26

I am the one and only

As ever I asked what I should write for you in this chapter. What came made me smile. It was only yesterday that I heard someone make reference to Chesney Hawks' hit "I am the One and Only!"...and today the message was repeated when I asked for my daily writing guidance, right away the chorus of the song rang through my head!

I am the one and only,
Nobody I'd rather be,
I am the one and only,
You can't take that away from me.

It reminded me of something I say often in my workshops, *"You can't be anyone else, because everyone else is already taken!"*

All too often we allow our inner critic to shout up and tell us all the things that we could be better at, to remind us of all of our shortcomings, and how rubbish we are.

Minute by minute, hour by hour, that's the soundtrack we're subjected to. I read a great passage in a book last night about just that topic; it asked if you would allow your best friend to talk to you with the same tone as your inner critic...I doubt they'd remain your best friend for very long...but then why do we tolerate such abuse from ourselves?

Well as of today your inner critic can take a holiday!

Today you're going to celebrate all the great things about YOU!

I'd like to urge you to take out a pen and a piece of paper now and following on from this statement, write down all of the fantastic things about YOU...

...I AM THE ONE AND ONLY...

And keep writing until your pen comes to rest...go ahead, celebrate, and capture YOU with all of your perfect, amazing, outstanding and remarkable talents...

Isn't it great to be you?

Wow, just look at all you are, all you bring to life. Others bring their gifts too, but you, well you're you, and there's nobody who can walk in your shoes. You're a perfect fit for the space that's called you. How does it feel?

Now, what if your inner critic went on a long haul holiday? Your inner critic has been around day in day out for years, probably since you were a very small child!

Isn't it about time your inner critic took a break?

Exercise: I am the one and only

Why not pack your inner critic off for a well deserved vacation, and whilst it's away maybe you could employ your inner "Number one fan" for a few weeks in replacement!

Imagine that; imagine if every day your inner number one fan was shouting you on, cheering from the sidelines, encouraging you every step of the way?

What would that feel like?

How might your inner number one fan talk to you?

How might it change your way of being?

Why not try it?

Every time you hear from your inner critic remind them, they're on holiday, but your inner number one fan is standing in for them.

Listen to your inner number one fan daily and I guarantee you'll experience such remarkable changes in your life you'll be sharing this quote from Lord Alan Sugar with your inner critic......

"You're fired!"

27

Going through the change?

Now as you read the title of this chapter, I can hear all the men saying, no, that chapter's not for me!

Wrong!

The change I'm talking about may well give you hot flushes and night sweats, but I'm not talking about the "M" word here...although men-o-pause, before you turn the page to the next chapter would be relevant!

Now, when I mention the word "Change" if it makes you feel a little nervous or uncomfortable, you aren't alone and certainly not unusual. Most of us like the comfort of our familiar routines, knowing where we are, and how we stand. Many even butt heads with change, fighting it every step of the way. Resisting what is only the natural flow of things.

Many people avoid too much in the way of change, in fact I see it all the time, especially in business, whilst there's talk of change, maybe some slight intent, more often, in truth it's much more common to hear "Why change, we've always done it that way", or "There's no point in change just for change's sake"

I'd like you to consider now any area of your life that is going through change.

Thought of one?

I'd hope so, because everything is changing in every second...really...think about it, whilst you're reading this, you're changing, you're different from a moment ago, since you've been reading this chapter you've been producing new skin cells, to replace old ones, your body has taken in new air and turned it into new energy...It's true! Now, let's take it a step further...How many babies do you think have been born into the world during the time it's taken you to read the last sentence?

Still think you're not going through the change?

You're on a journey, an adventure of constant change, where in actual fact the only thing that is constant is change itself!

So, if you and I and everyone and everything is in a constant state of "Going through the change" maybe we should see it as a constant friend, something we can rely on?

With change comes opportunity, we are always evolving into something new, a newer enhanced version of ourselves.

What upgraded and newer version of yourself would you like to be?

If you're going to be "Going through the change" in any case, why not put your heart and soul into it?

What would you change right now?

How would you change right now?

If you were putting your heart and soul, your purest intent into your evolution what would be different?

So, as you "Go through the change" I'd like you to consider seeing it not as hot flushes and night sweats, something to bemoan or act as a signpost for the frustrations of change.

No, instead of fighting against the most certain aspect of your life, I'd like you to consider that "Going through the change" is the journey of you unfolding perfectly, in perfect time, always!

Exercise: Going through the change

Where in your life are you experiencing the greatest change right now?

What growth and learning is this opportunity giving you?

How can you better embrace this change?

28

Feeling the pinch?

Interesting term don't you think?

"Feeling the pinch". Everywhere you look right now we're flooded with negativity around the "economic climate", despite the fact that we're now out of recession – every newspaper, every radio station, every television station, the internet and even your next-door neighbour is still talking about it, thinking about it and feeling it! I just read the latest excellent article by Liz Villani, she talks about this very same topic but from a much more positive perspective...we get what we focus on; like placing an order if you like, with the cosmic warehouse...Which inspired me to write this chapter (Thanks Liz!).

So if our thoughts and emotions create our reality...why focus thoughts and feelings on more of what you don't want??????? What I find most interesting; and those of you who know me will understand this, is that if we build up this negativity and allow ourselves to be swept along with the doom and gloom merchants, very soon we are "Feeling the pinch" ourselves...and not just in our wallets or purses!

Our body is constantly having a conversation with us, if you ignore what your body's trying to tell you, before you know it, it will make you listen by "Feeling the pinch" quite literally! Be it trapped nerves in your back (needing more support, and financial worries) to tension in your shoulders (carrying emotional and financial burdens), to a cricked neck (what or who is your pain in the neck)... to name but a few! The stress and negative emotions we hold in our bodies eventually will manifest as aches and pains if we don't take note. By being more aware of where we're putting our focus we really can help or hinder ourselves! So ask yourself:

Are you half full?
Or Are you half empty?

The health benefits of a positive outlook are well-researched and proven! Those with a positive outlook have a greater resistance to catching the common cold, have a reduced risk of coronary artery disease, display better coping skills during hardships and have a greater sense of wellness.

So how about challenging yourself to be more positive?

Here are two little challenges for you!

1. The positivity challenge:

For the week, every time you make a negative statement or have a negative thought, STOP! Take a moment...then rephrase it into a positive! Before you know it you'll be promoting positive thoughts, actions and feelings...and actively improving your health and wellness!

2. SMILE
If you find yourself without a smile then it's easy…

JUST SMILE

then stop

now JUST SMILE

then stop

now JUST SMILE

by the third time of smiling your brain actually thinks you're smiling for real and starts to release happy hormones into the body! If that's not enough to get you cracking a smile...

Top 10 Reasons To Smile. Smiling is a great way to make yourself stand out while helping your body to function better. Smile to improve your health, your stress level, and your attractiveness.

1. Smiling makes us attractive.
We are drawn to people who smile. There is an attraction factor. We want to know a smiling person and figure out what is so good. Frowns, scowls and grimaces all push people away–but a smile draws them in.

2. Smiling Changes Our Mood.
Next time you are feeling down, try putting on a smile. There's a good chance your mood will change for the better. Smiling can trick the body into helping you change your mood.

3. Smiling is Contagious.
When someone is smiling they lighten up the room, change the moods of others, and make things happier. A smiling person brings happiness with them. Smile lots and you will draw people to you.

4. Smiling Relieves Stress.
Stress can really show up in our faces. Smiling helps to prevent us from looking tired, worn down, and overwhelmed. When you are stressed, take time to put on a smile. The stress should be reduced and you'll be better able to take action.

5. Smiling Boosts Your Immune System.
Smiling helps the immune system to work better. When you

smile, immune function improves possibly because you are more relaxed. Prevent the flu and colds by smiling.

6. Smiling Lowers Your Blood Pressure.
When you smile, there is a measurable reduction in your blood pressure. Give it a try if you have a blood pressure monitor at home. Sit for a few minutes, take a reading. Then smile for a minute and take another reading while still smiling. Do you notice a difference?

7. Smiling Releases Endorphins, Natural Pain Killers and Serotonin.
Studies have shown that smiling releases endorphins, natural pain killers, and serotonin. Together these three make us feel good. Smiling is a natural drug.

8. Smiling Lifts the Face and Makes You Look Younger.
The muscles we use to smile lift the face, making a person appear younger. Don't go for a face lift, just try smiling your way through the day–you'll look younger and feel better.

9. Smiling Makes You Seem Successful.
Smiling people appear more confident, are more likely to be promoted, and more likely to be approached. Put on a smile at meetings and appointments and people will react to you differently.

10. Smiling Helps You Stay Positive.
Try this test: Smile. Now try to think of something negative without losing the smile. It's hard. When we smile our body is sending the rest of us a message that "Life is Good!" Stay away from depression, stress and worry by smiling.

So go ahead, SMILE!

29

The Neg heads

From time to time it's inevitable that you will come across "The Neg heads". It's just part and parcel of the journey. By the Neg heads of course I'm talking about those people who choose to take a negative viewpoint in their day to day lives. You'll recognise them through their body language, the energy they give off and their use of language.

Now understand, I'm not judging the Neg heads, in fact, more often than not, I strive to understand how they come to be that way. That's always something to consider when faced with a Neg head. What is going on in their world that means they see the world in such a negative way, instead of enjoying the amazing gifts life in this world can offer.

However, when faced with a Neg head, one of two things can happen. You can either match their energy, or they can match yours. That is you can infect them with enthusiasm, or be dragged down to their way of thinking. And it is just that...a way of thinking. You choose your thoughts in any situation, that is the gift of being human. Even in the most challenging and difficult situations you can choose to be "Half full" or "Half empty".

Should you encounter a Neg head that tries to drag you down, I sometimes call them a dream stealer (as opposed to a dream maker) well, I'd challenge you to understand why.

What is going on for them, that they feel the need to project their negativity onto you?

Are they in a place of Love?

Or in a place of Fear?

No one can make you feel inferior without your consent. ~ Eleanor Roosevelt

The other thing to consider and I'm sure I've mentioned this before, is that thoughts become things, so if you have a Neg head around you, and you focus on the fact that they are always negative, what are they going to be?

So see the very best in people and they will demonstrate more of that to you! Try it, it works!

Another tip a good friend of mine once gave me was, when faced with a Neg head, think or say "Peace be with you", as every thought has a vibration and thoughts become things, it can't fail to work!

And here's another thought, what if you happen one day to be a Neg head?

What will you do to change your thoughts?

Simply choose to change your thoughts to a positive!

Exercise: The Neg heads

Today I urge you to list down everything you're feeling negative about.

For each negative statement, now take a moment to reword every phrase into a positive.

Notice how differently you feel.

30

Rainbows

Don't miss all the beautiful colours of the rainbow looking for that pot of gold.

From as early a time as I can remember, I have had a fascination with rainbows. As a child I would walk for miles with my best friend so we could try and reach the end of the rainbow and the pot of gold. Somehow we were never discouraged by the rainbow that kept on moving, the pot of gold always elusive. It was an adventure we simply didn't grow weary of.

There's simply something magical about rainbows, of course they are a result of prismatic effect, but more than that for me they hold all the colours in the light spectrum, they represent all the colours of the chakras (esoteric energy centres) and most significantly to me, they symbolise a bridge, between heaven and Earth.

Now I'm not talking of heaven with white bearded man sat on a cloud (but if that works for you, then that's fine). I'm meaning a bridge between the infinite and the present moment, the limitless possibility in every moment, right NOW to create heaven on Earth.

Most of the colours that you and I see are produced by part of the sun's light energy being absorbed/smothered by the objects around us. The red chair, say, gives far less light energy than it receives, whereas the heavenly principle is to GIVE **AS** WE RECEIVE. To consider light and colour from a spiritual viewpoint we should look at colour by transmitted light. These colours are, of course, the colours of the rainbow, when no light is lost but its inner beauties are quite literally opened out before our eyes as it shines through the transparent water droplets in the rain cloud. We are not intended to absorb the light...enlightenment, joy and happiness...rather we are intended to transmit it; and in doing so to unfold its meaning for others, and for ourselves too.

The colours of the rainbow are not just wonderful images in our natural world but also convey deep meaning.

As a child I loved to play with fuzzy felt, creating countryside scenes, stretching out to the horizon, my creations always included the sun and a rainbow.

I also loved chalking on the slabs outside the door, again I always created rainbows. Even now if I see a rainbow I just have to stop and more often than not I take a photograph.

Did you know that the colours of the rainbow have deep effects on us, each colour has a different frequency, a different vibration that interacts with our energy. Maybe that explains my fascination with rainbows?

Do you recall the song "I can sing a rainbow"? I always thought it odd as a child that the lyrics asked you to listen with your eyes and hear everything you see...but now I appreciate that all of our senses are stimulated by the rainbow.

So when you see a rainbow, stop and take in its symbolism, its magnificence, beauty and magic.

Remember there's no need to chase the pot of gold as the greatest gift is contained within the rainbow its self, think about it... the gift after rain with a bow on it!

31

Shakti

This chapter came about after a series of synchronicities. For a few weeks now I have been "Tweeting" with a lovely Swedish woman living in London. She has a company that distributes and sells Shakti mats.

It struck me how much we seemed to just get along, even in the world of Twitter. Intrigued, I clicked onto her website and read all about the amazing product, then I clicked through to read some more. It was when I got to the history that I started to smile...It hadn't really struck me before despite having shared messages for some weeks, the deep connection between the basis of our work. The connection was Shakti.

The word "Shakti" is a Sanskrit word meaning sacred force or empowerment, is the primordial cosmic energy and represents the dynamic forces that move through the entire universe. Shakti is the concept, or personification, of divine feminine creative power, sometimes referred to as "The Great Divine Mother" in Hinduism. It symbolises female power, compassion, and the nurturing, warm, creative spark within all of us.

It was so interesting to find that we were singing the same song, just presenting it in different ways.

It reminded me that regardless of being male or female, we all have that creative energy within us, that if cultivated holds the energy of infinite possibility. If we are able to truly nurture that creative spark, we not only have the whole World in our hands, but the force of the Universe by our side.

How do you cultivate your creative spark?

Do you allow yourself to be creative?

In workshops I often come across participants, both men and

women who say that they're just simply not creative.

True, some people are more disposed to right or left brain dominance. But by nature we are all creative, every single one of us. It's more about how you define creativity.

cre·a·tive

adj.

1. Having the ability or power to create: Human beings are creative animals.

2. Productive; creating.

3. Characterised by originality and expressiveness; imaginative: creative writing.

n.

One who displays productive originality.

We all have a toolkit and palette to work from, we all have the inbuilt ability to create. But then why do some of us create a masterpiece from our life and others not?

Now I say masterpiece, that's a good point to look at in more detail.

What makes a masterpiece?

If we liken this to art for just a moment. For some a masterpiece may be a renaissance painting, for another it may be an abstract piece of art. Another may see "masterpiece" in an impressionist's work. All are different, all are masterpieces of creative spark and genius, but what is seen as a masterpiece to one person may appear as insignificant to another.

The point I'm making here is this. We have the creative spark (Shakti) within us to create our own masterpiece of a life. It's YOUR masterpiece, your creation. You choose the canvas, the materials, the colours and the style with which you make your mark. But don't ever doubt that if you think you're creative, or you think you're not, YOU ARE creating every single moment, of every single day.

Exercise: Are you creating a masterpiece?

Consider this...What masterpiece are you creating?

What's missing from your masterpiece?

What else could you include in your masterpiece?

32

Heart song

Always be a first-rate version of yourself, instead of a second-rate version of somebody else
~ Judy Garland

I was talking earlier with a friend of mine and during the conversation the word "Imitation" was used. It stimulated the thought for today's chapter (along with another about Shakti).

I wanted to talk to you today, about being the "real deal" and accepting no imitations. I often talk about just this topic in my workshops, asking participants to consider if they're being the full version of themselves. It can be quite a challenging question to answer, as in truth as human beings we are constantly in a state of being "a work in progress".

But it's still a great question to ask yourself, as it provokes a deep response if asked of yourself with an open heart and total honesty.

Are you living the full version of yourself, without exception?

Or are you being the imitation of yourself...

im·i·ta·tion *n.*
1. The act or an instance of imitating.
2. Something derived or copied from an original.
adj. Made to resemble another, usually superior material.

So often we try to fit into a role that is to someone else's specification, design and fit. We try on this role for size, but it doesn't quite fit, it's a little uncomfortable in places, it might pinch a little, be too restrictive... but still it'll do...won't it?

I understand that sometimes we have to realise who we aren't, to know truly who we are!

Just like Mr Benn; for those old enough to remember, it is actually great fun hitting the dressing-up box and trying on costumes for size, figuring out who you are, what you value, how you express yourself can be so much fun...But if we're to become the full version of ourselves we have to be true and authentic to who we really are at heart.

I urge you to consider right now, where you're wearing someone else's shoes, where in your life are things not quite fitting you anymore...

Then jump into the changing room of life and true Wonder Woman or Superman style...become your own super hero, (don't worry I'm not suggesting you wear your underpants on the outside of your trousers...unless that's your authentic self of course). Move towards making the changes to be more of yourself, the full and bright sparkling version in glorious Technicolor!

Are you feeling courageous?
Are you feeling empowered?
Are you feeling brave?

NOW...if you're ready...make a vow to be YOU, the real YOU and nothing but YOU!

It's liberating to sing your own heart song, you'll never be out of tune, the harmony will always be spot on, and you'll be a number one hit, for yourself, your family, friends, employer, everyone and most of all, do you know what? Everything will just FIT!

It takes courage to grow up and become who you really are
~ E. E. Cummings

33

Ho'oponopono

"Whom do you need to forgive?"

Have you someone you need to forgive? It may seem a hard question for some of you, if it strikes a chord with you, if you feel a rising emotion when I ask that question; does the emotion you feel come from Love or Fear?

Maybe you feel someone has wronged you? That you have to hold onto anger, resentment, hurt, pain...but when you do, where are you holding onto those emotions and what effect are they having on you?

One thing I can say for sure, the person you are holding a grudge about won't be feeling the emotion or pain you're feeling.

In letting go and releasing negative fear-based emotion and allowing yourself to forgive, you're loving yourself. Holding onto the negative fear based emotion just keeps you stuck, it keeps you in the past as you associate with the event or action that caused your anger, frustration or resentment in the first place. You are simply only hurting yourself. If you loved yourself enough to forgive...what would that feel like? What would it feel like to cut the ties that bind you?

The art of forgiveness is a liberating experience. It makes me recall a beautiful Huna prayer "HoAoponopono" (ho-o-pono-pono) is an ancient Hawaiian practice of reconciliation and forgiveness.

Ho'oponopono - a tool for life...

Ho'oponopono really is an incredible tool. And tool is probably the right word for it, because what ho'oponopono does most is *help*. Isn't that the definition of a tool? Something that helps?

What is it then that makes ho'oponopono (ho oponopono, hooponopono) so exceptional?

Ho'oponopono is extremely simple to do.

Despite its simplicity, ho'oponopono has very broad uses that become increasingly apparent the more you use it.

Using ho'oponopono leads to profound results.

Exercise: Ho'opnopono

How to do ho'oponopono

How does a person use ho'oponopono?

Say the following:

I love you, I'm sorry, please forgive me, thank you.

Say this phrase silently to yourself, say it as often as possible and preferably say it all the time.

Is silently saying "I love you, I'm sorry, please forgive me, thank you" all there is to ho'oponopono?

No, it can go broader than that. My experience is that as people use ho'oponopono, they seek more information about it and their application of the technique expands and they become better at it. But silently saying "I love you, I'm sorry, please forgive me, thank you" is ho'oponopono and it does work.

Expectations with ho'oponopono.

One of the more important elements of using ho'oponopono, something I believe really needs to be emphasised, is not having expectations for an outcome.

For instance, a person uses ho'oponopono then sits back and says, "Okay, now I want this particular thing to happen in my life" is not the way ho'oponopono works. Using ho'oponopono is not the equivalent of ordering something from the universe. Engaging the ho'oponopono method is to erase, and to invite inspiration and guidance from the highest source.

When you use ho'oponopono, *let go*. Don't attempt to dictate. Don't attempt to direct. Let go of your ego expectations, and allow yourself to be carried down a gentle, loving stream.

Know this: all the answers that you need are within you. Use ho'oponopono earnestly and you'll get the answers and the help that you need.

34

Namaste, Shalom, Aloha

Last Friday I was blessed to run another Get a Life workshop. This time it was "Create your vision – manifest your best life!". It was a beautiful sunny day on Friday, the venue was the tranquil Welland Enterprise offices, which nestle in the Lincolnshire countryside, certainly a far fling from the hustle and bustle of most daily lives.

Again, as always on my workshops, I was blessed by being surrounded by an amazing group of participants for the day, the energy amongst the group was fantastic. Each one open, caring and sharing with one another on their journey.

It was as a result of a discussion during one of the exercises on Friday that I thought about the topic for today's blog.

During the session we discussed life as a journey...considering if we were "hurtling along a motorway or meandering along a wooded lane..."

Were we taking the opportunity to savour every juicy moment or were we just rushing to the destination, without enjoying the scenery along the way?

Did we stop and "Gather the rose buds will ye may?"

Did we take the opportunity to connect and re-connect with those who shared the road?

I urge you to consider this:

How many people do you connect with, no matter how briefly throughout your day?

Are you truly present with each? Or are you in a hurry to move on and on along your motorway?

What would happen if you took the opportunity to slow down just enough to really connect or in truth re-connect with those other souls?

I say re-connect because I don't believe there really is a such a distance between us all, right at the very heart of us we're not so very different are we? We may have lots of variations but we're human beings, trying not to be just human doings!

How do you greet those along your path?

Do you stop long enough to share the gifts you may have for one another?

What nuggets and gems do you miss each day by rushing on past?

You may have seen the greeting/salutation "Namaste" used by myself and others...this simple word captures so much of what I'm talking about here:

NAMASTE – one translation of this ancient Sanskrit word is – "I honour the place in you in which the entire Universe dwells, I honour the place in you which is of Love, of Integrity, of Wisdom and of Peace. When you are in that place in you, and I am in that place in me, we are One."

Other cultures have similar greetings:

SHALOM – The Hebrew word *SHALOM* is understood around the world to mean peace. But peace is only one small part of the meaning of the word *SHALOM,* it also expresses completeness, wholeness, health, welfare, safety soundness, tranquillity, prosperity, perfectness, fullness, rest, harmony, the absence of agitation or discord. So by using this greeting/salutation we are showing the intent of this expression to the receiver.

ALOHA – Aloha is an Hawaiian greeting, it has an essence of love weaved within it. Aloha is a way of being and of living...its true meaning is better captured here:

Aloha is being a part of all, and all being a part of me. When there is pain – it is my pain. When there is joy – it is also mine. I respect all that is as part of the Creator and part of me. I will not wilfully harm anyone or anything. When food is needed I will take only my need and explain why it is being taken. The earth, the sky, the sea are mine to care for, to cherish and to protect – this is Aloha!

When you stop to consider the depth of meaning contained within these greetings. It makes you consider what an amazing gift they bring between two souls. The simple act of greeting another has profound energy and effect.

HELLO may not, on the face of it hold such significant meaning when shared, however the intent of hello is to acknowledge another, that in itself shows care, respect and recognition.

Exercise: Hello!

So today as you walk along your journey, I urge you slow down enough to connect with the other souls walking alongside you, no matter if your greeting is Namaste, Shalom, Aloha or a simple hello, don't miss the opportunity to connect and share.

It's the enjoyment of the journey that counts, moment to moment...

35

The living moment

The living moment is everything
~ D.H. Lawrence

Well, I woke up this morning to the sun streaming through the window, I thought to myself, wow! A beautiful brand new day full of moments to live and experience!

Strange, though, that as I went to sleep last night, I had a recall of Sunday nights when I was in the corporate world, I have to admit that back then, going to sleep knowing I had the JOB to do the next morning would fill me with an overwhelming oppressive feeling. I went on to dream I was back there, in my corporate clone life...how very strange...So how timely that I should be prompted to write today's blog!

I guess last night's dream added to my delight this morning, when I woke to a bright sunshiny day of moments to be "on purpose", fully aware, fully awake to the day's opportunity.

A lot has changed for me since those days of being on the corporate hamster wheel, going through the motions, going around and around, until I was lulled into a corporate clone existence.

I have learned so much, but if I can be bold enough to share with you the greatest learning since that time...

Yes, I am now living "on purpose" as I have stated, I am living a life that allows me to be the full version of myself, without exception. I can be my own boss, I can take breaks when I wish, but that's not the only reason I am joyful when I wake.

I have learnt this...I have a choice!

I have a choice to be happy.

I have a choice to be fully aware and awake.

I have a choice to be mindful in every juicy moment.

No matter what I'm doing, no matter where I am, that choice comes from within me.

Have you ever driven from home to a familiar location, only to arrive in a haze, without any recollection of the journey?

That's a great metaphor of how so many of us live our lives!

But it doesn't have to be like that.

You have a choice.

In fact, here's a little exercise to test out how much you're aware and awake and living mindfully in this moment. Close your eyes and picture the shoes you put on this morning. Take in every little detail, from the colour to the design, any scuffs or marks...

Now open your eyes and compare what you thought your shoes were like, to how they actually are...notice how many little differences you can spot?

That little glimpse into how aware and unaware we can be from moment to moment! This little exercise is simple, being aware of the shoes that are on your very on feet, carrying you through your day and your life!

I use it to make a point...are you bumbling along in a daze? Or are you mindful of every moment, of everyone and everything around you and your connection to it?

I'm sure you really concentrated on the details of your shoes whilst your eyes were closed, but imagine how in real life we bumble along in a daze, so much is changing in every moment and we're not even noticing!

Exercise: The living moment

So, here's a little tip, try this...

Start by finding yourself somewhere where you can sit quietly and where you won't be disturbed.

Close your eyes and take three deep breaths, be mindful of every detail of the breath, moving in and out, be aware of the rise and fall of your chest.

Now open your eyes and choose a point of reference right in front of you...a small point, look really hard at it, just that point, focus your complete attention on that point, notice every detail of that point.

After a few moments, still focusing on that point, become aware of what is just to the left and right of it, then become aware of what is just above and below it. All of the time keeping your focus on the point, after a few moments more, you can expand your awareness further to the left and the right, above and below, whilst still focusing directly at the point.

Keep expanding further and further...be aware of what is on the edges of your field of vision, all of the time focusing on the spot.

Now see with your mind's eye what is behind you above you and below you, still keeping your focus on the point ahead. When you are ready return to your normal visual field, notice how your level of awareness and connection to all around you has increased, and the detail amplified???

Sometimes it's a simple acknowledgement that you've "drifted off" that will bring you back to mindfulness in the present moment...It can be as simple as being present and actively noticing the interaction your have with everything and everyone around your through your six senses...yes that's right! I did say six...your intuitive sense is included in being fully alive and living in this moment.

So no matter what is going on in your world, you can make the choice to live in each moment and make every single juicy moment count.

After all Life is taking place moment by moment...why would you want to let life pass you by without living it?

Life is what happens while you are busy making other plans
~ John Lennon

36

Spice up your life

There are shortcuts to happiness, and dancing is one of them
~ Vicki Baum

I must give credit to John Armitage; a therapist friend of mine, for the title of this chapter. It came to in a flash of inspiration as we were talking about another topic. So, whilst pondering what to write today, the title came back to me.

I was reminded of a time when I listened to *The Spice Girls* singing a song of the very same title. I must admit I felt like dancing around the office, just at the memory of it! The song reminds me of a great time of "girl power" and also of a great group of empowered young women I was working with at the time.

As I recalled the lyrics, this line jumped out at me...All you need is positivity!

It's so true, no matter how sad or low you may feel, music has the ability to shift you!

In this case the uplifting "Spice up your Life!", but the lyrics do have a point...Smiling and dancing is free, and you just do need positivity to shift from sad and low to a spiced-up life.

That's not to say that a difficult situation disappears, but it does appear differently as a result.

I must admit, I have some favourite songs that if I'm having a down moment I put on to play and turn up loud!

I find smiling and dancing really moves stagnant, stuck energy and throw in a pinch of laughter and you've a recipe for an uplifting mood shift.

And do you know what, there are other benefits to smiling

and dancing too...

Smiling Makes Us Attractive We are drawn to people who smile. There is an attraction factor. We want to know a smiling person and figure out what is so good.

Smiling Changes Our Mood. Next time you are feeling down, try putting on a smile. There's a good chance you mood will change for the better.

Smiling can trick the body into helping you change your mood.

Smiling Is Contagious When someone is smiling they lighten up the room, change the moods of others, and make things happier.

A smiling person brings happiness with them. Smile lots and you will draw people to you.

Smiling Releases Endorphins, Natural Pain Killers and Serotonin Studies have shown that smiling releases endorphins, natural pain killers, and serotonin. Together these three make us feel good. Smiling is a natural drug.

Dancing is a social activity. Studies have shown that strong social ties and socialising with friends contribute to high self-esteem and a positive outlook. Because physical activity reduces stress and tension, regular dancing gives an overall sense of well-being.

You can dance anywhere, even if only in your heart
~ Author Unknown

As the Spice Girls themselves told us...the power is in our hands...or feet should I say...

Power to the world...Spice up your life!

If your life is listless and lacking in energy (E-motion) why not try Spicing it up a little with a little song and dance...

Why not try it now...get the rest of the office dancing, dance around your kitchen...dance down the street with the kids on it'll put a smile on your face and a bounce in your step...and then something magic happens...suddenly Life feels altogether better.

Dancing is like dreaming with your feet!
~ Constanze

Make every moment count...and go ahead, Spice up your life!

Dance, even if you have nowhere to do it but your living room
~ Kurt Vonnegut

Exercise: Spice up your life

Today, I urge you to capture all the ways you have "Spiced up your life!"

37

What you focus on grows

A man is but the product of his thoughts; what he thinks, he becomes ~ Mahatma Gandhi

I just had to share with you, today I heard a cool new video offering from The and Leakster; (Get Spanky - what you focus on grows) I had the great pleasure of meeting Barefoot Doctor just the other week and was totally inspired!

What you focus on grows!

(Or you may have heard me say, where focus goes, energy flows)

Thoughts Become Things because thoughts ***are*** things

Thoughts are the DNA, the building materials, if you like, of the universe, and the universe is made entirely of energy in its many forms. Thoughts become things when they are sparked into life by heartfelt emotion. (Emotion as in E-motion, energy in motion).

Belief is thinking that is given meaning and direction by the mind using the power of that emotion – **Energy in Motion**.

It is this energy in motion and the resulting vibrational domino effect on all surrounding energy (the universe around us) that gives life to the thought and this causes physical manifestation and experience to take place. That is the thought comes to life!

The energy in motion (E-motion) powers the thought into action (physical manifestation) regardless of the positive or negative charge of that emotion. And where does the positive or negative charge come from? Your Beliefs!

Positive = Empowering   Negative = Limiting

So how are thoughts and beliefs formed?

Well from all of the data we compute and store in our subconscious mind. What we're told and taught from an early age by: our parents, our family, our friends, school, community, the news and media...everything around us.

But we have a choice – in fact we have a RESPONSIBILITY

For every thought we have, we can choose to add a Positive or Negative charge! (What you focus on grows regardless, so why would you choose a negative charge when you can choose a positive?)

It's simple...we have the ABILITY to choose our RESPONSE (Responsibility)

I could go on and on here about just how to choose the positive outlook, to choose Love over Fear, but that's a full workshop in itself!

But thanks to The Barefoot Doctor you now have a simple reminder...

"What you focus on grows"

Turning dreams into reality.

"I will achieve the best that I aim to believe in!" Your mind is yours to conduct. Only you can choose if you will feed it with fruit or poison. (Positive or negative thoughts and beliefs). You are what you "think" yourself to be. It is never too late to alter direction. It is never too late to paint a new picture for your life. You're creating it moment by moment! You're a work in progress an artist in your own right!

Exercise: What you focus on grows

So today I urge you to choose to focus on the great thoughts, the positive thoughts and loving thoughts and powered by heartfelt emotion, do you know what will happen? They will begin to manifest and grow right in front of your eyes!

As you focus more and more why not capture your manifested thoughts?

38

Love is...

Love is...Finding a rose on the car seat.

Well, no doubt I'm just about to show my age with this chapter...In fact some of my readers may be forgiven for being too young to even remember what I'm about to talk about, nevertheless, I feel the reference is a worthwhile lead into the most meaningful topic of all.

LOVE.

Out of the blue, and I have no idea why, I just recalled an image from my childhood. I guess I would have been around 7 or 8 years old or so when there was a huge craze sweeping across the country for sticker books.

The idea being, you would purchase the sticker book, then collect packets of stickers to fill your book, swapping prize stickers with others when you found yourself with duplicates...a great marketing idea I guess. Now, not to appear sexist, as I'm not...mostly I recall the boys collected Panini stickers...filling their time swapping stickers of key football stars (my Dad encouraged me to collect these too, but I feel that it was more to his benefit than mine, truth be told!)...whilst the girls, myself included, collected "Love is..." stickers (of course I'm sure there were some exceptions to the girl/boy purchasing habits).

I've googled the images…it seems whilst football stickers live on right at the top of the search rankings...sadly the days of the "Love is..." are a distant memory along with Holly Hobby (see told you it would show my age) and took a long search to find.

I think it's kind of sad really that children are no longer collecting symbols of what Love is all about...I know maybe I'm being a bit soppy...It was after all a marketer's dream...all those little girls collecting stickers week after week with their pocket money...but surely collecting positive affirmations about Love is a good thing?

It got me to thinking...what words were on those stickers?

I really can't recall the exact phrases, but what I do recall was the simple messages that Love is in everything, every smile, every kind word, every kind deed done for another.

I wonder how many relationships would benefit with a little trip down memory lane...just to recall stickers such as...

"Love is...being able to keep cool when he makes the floors dirty just after you have cleaned them."

or **"Love is...leaving love messages into the drawers of the desk."**

or maybe **" Love is...counting until 10 instead of shouting."**

Simple acts of love admittedly, but that's just the point...Love isn't difficult...in fact Love is the most natural emotion we can have.

Exercise: Love is....

So today I urge you to take just a moment to consider just what Love is.

And if you feel inclined, why not capture them here?

I'll start you off if you like...

Love is...Saying those three little words to the ones who mean the most.

I LOVE YOU !

39

Marvellous Monday

mar·vel·ous also **mar·vel·lous** (märv-ls)

adj. **1.** Causing wonder or astonishment. **2.** Miraculous; supernatural. **3.** Of the highest or best kind or quality; first-rate.

According to the news this morning, today has been named the most miserable day of the year, triggered by bad weather, money worries and failed resolutions. Termed "Blue Monday" today is reported to be the worst day of the year. But is it?

Ok I understand all of the rationale behind the claim, but surely today is what we choose it to be?

Today is a gift...a huge present waiting to be unwrapped.

Today is what you choose and believe it to be – it's true!

Now if you choose to subscribe to the "Blue Monday" label...then guess what? It will be.

If you choose to subscribe to my title "Marvellous Monday" then hey presto, your wish is your command (See what I did there?).

Now I posted on Facebook about this very topic and in the main, most people agreed with my idea that it's all about choice and belief. The odd one had had a few blips to the start of their day, but to them I suggested they try shifting their attention and focus to the great things that were happening around and within them today, because for sure there would be some.

"Where focus goes, energy flows"

So today I would ask you to detox – Yes detox your mind, let go of any negative and limiting beliefs about today. Instead marvel in the miraculous gift that is opening and unfolding before you.

If you feel yourself being drawn into the swell of "Blue Monday" just take a breath, take a moment now to breathe really deeply for a few minutes and feel the tension slip away. Next smile and keep on smiling, it really works, it kids your brain you're smiling for real, even if you're "Acting as if" and your body will do all the necessary work, releasing a surge of happy hormones, resulting in your feeling happy!

Here's another idea for you – why not take a walk outside?

It's amazing how we can get cooped up in the house or the office in the Wintertime...getting some fresh air to blow away the cobwebs; so to speak, allowing yourself some fresh air and scenery, can give you a whole new perspective.

Think of something you have to look forwards to. It can be anything, big or small. It gives you a sense of purpose and also a point of perspective.

Make a wish – dream a dream – imagine...

Turn your focus to the bright star that is your future, buck the trend, why follow the crowd?

So choose to have a Marvellous Monday...choose to have a marvellous everyday for that matter !

Today is just a perfect day!

If you choose it to be so – in the words of the very amazing Lou Reed "You're gonna reap just what you sow"

Sow those seeds of thought wisely.

Exercise: Marvellous Monday

Take a moment to note down all of the marvellous things that have occurred for you in your day.

40

Don't worry about a thing

As I wondered and pondered what to write about today. I pulled "Relax – everything's ok" from my oracle cards and the instant I did the Bob Marley song came to mind!

"Don't worry about a thing, cause every little thing is going to be ok."

Sometimes we just hit a slump, maybe a grey day outside, sometimes we lose sight of that New Year inspiration that we started out with on the 1st of January. You know that "new page" feeling that you have as a new year begins, full of hope, inspiration and good intent.

I don't know about you, but I almost want to fill that blank page with all the bursting ideas that I have at the dawning of a new year, as quickly as I possibly can . And that's the point...capturing the dreams and ideas is exactly what's required at this point in the year, but without the rush.

> *The act of putting pen to paper encourages pause for thought, this in turn makes us think more deeply about life, which helps us regain our equilibrium*
> *~ Norbet Platt*

We then hit the middle of the month and that "Joie de Vie" may be waning a little. Sometimes I find myself feeling a sense of urgency to "Get on" and "Get going". But I do realise sometimes I forget to take a breath!

There's a whole lifetime to bring my dreams alive, sometimes even I have to remind myself that.

I had a quick listen to Bob Marley, just the Reggae beat lifted my spirits, his music bringing the sound of sun into the room!

I guess I really just needed to hit the "Pause" button for a moment and take a breath, we can so easily set off into the year as though its a 100m sprint...that just leads to burn out!

If I take a look outside my window, the garden is still sleeping, yes of course underground the Earth is getting ready for the season to come, but it's still resting, regenerating and gaining its energy in readiness for the spring season.

Sometimes I have to take a look at nature to get back into rhythm, to honour my body and the cycle of things. It reminds me that now is the time for making the plans, taking the choices and tending to the resources needed. It's all about planning now...action comes later.

What's the hurry, what's the rush, start slow and finish strong!

He who can no longer pause to wonder and stand rapt in awe, is as good as dead; his eyes are closed
~ Albert Einstein

Everything happens in perfect time – always.

So, if you find that the energy that you set off with at the start of the year, month, week, day...is unsustainable and you're worrying that you're loosing momentum, just remember it's all about pacing yourself. You can't run the year as a 100m sprint, besides why would you want to?

Allow for the pause.
Nothing is spoiling.
Everything is unfolding perfectly,
Just as it should.

It is in those moments of pause the messages come, the signs and the symbols, if you're sprinting through your year, you'll simply miss them.

Allow yourself time to pause for thought, allow yourself to dream your dreams. The time for planning is now. Don't worry about a thing...

Let our advance worrying become advance thinking and planning ~ Winston Churchill

Exercise: Taking a breath

Today I urge you to sit quietly for five whole minutes at some point in your busy schedule and simply breathe...just breathe, do nothing, think nothing...just breathe...

What do you notice having done this?

41

Make a choice

So where are you in your year?

How's it been so far?

Maybe you've charged ahead already, or maybe you've just drifted out of last year and found yourself halfway into the next year, with no real purpose or direction.

Time keeps moving on, you can choose to make something of it, or you can continue doing and being just as you were before.

> *You've got a lot of choices. If getting out of bed in the morning is a chore and you're not smiling on a regular basis, try another choice ~ Steven D. Woodhull*

Now staying in your comfort zone is maybe familiar, safe and known.

But what would happen if you chose to move out of your comfort zone into your opportunity zone?

> *I held a moment in my hand, brilliant as a star, fragile as a flower, a tiny sliver of one hour. I dripped it carelessly. Ah! I didn't know, I held opportunity ~ Hazel Lee*

It would require you to make a choice, a choice to step into the unknown of course, but just imagine if your were just brave enough, if you trusted that inner voice, amazing things could occur.

What would it feel like if your were to follow your own heart song?

If you dared to be you, the whole version of you what choice would you make today?

What would you do if you knew you couldn't fail?

Now you may have heard me say there's no such thing as failure, only feedback...and it's true!

If you knew right now that no matter what choice you make it can't end in failure only success and feedback...then what could possibly stop you from making choices that allowed you to be more YOU?

Of course if you think about it, you can't help making a choice, in every moment, from one moment to the next. Even if you think you're not making a choice, you of course are. You're making a choice not to chose...and that in itself is a choice!

> *When you have to make a choice and don't make it, that is in itself a choice ~ William James*

By making a conscious choice you are calling your spirit home. You are allowing your song to be sung, you are opening yourself up to the limitless opportunity that lies within you.

Choices are the hinges of destiny.

What dreams do you have that are as yet unmet?

What has stopped you from perusing them?

Start now, today, make a choice to bring that dream alive once more. Set out on the journey, every step leads to big dreams...

The journey of a thousand miles begins with a single step.

Listen to your heart song...is it playing your song, or that of another?

Sing YOUR song, sing loud, sing proud.

Make a choice today...Make a choice and follow your dreams.

Exercise: Following your dreams

What dreams do you hold, that as yet you haven't fulfilled?

What stops you from making your dreams come true?

What would you need to change to move closer to your dreams?

What action will you take to move towards at least one of your dreams today?

About the author

The Soul Purpose Coach - Opening hearts & changing lives

Positivity expert
Multi-award winning therapist
Natural intuitive
Inspirational and Motivational Speaker
Coach and Mentor

Lisa Whitehead is a Soul purpose coach and mentor with many years' experience in understanding people and how they grow and develop. For over 20 years Lisa worked within blue chip organisations, such as the Sears group, The Boots company and Barclays bank, before taking the leap of faith to follow her heart and be true to her own Soul purpose.

Lisa is a natural intuitive and a highly qualified therapist which enables her to really connect with her clients, understanding each person as a whole. Lisa truly engages people to "Do what makes their heart sing and spirit soar"!

www.getalife-uk.co.uk

O is a symbol of the world, of oneness and unity. In different cultures it also means the "eye," symbolizing knowledge and insight. We aim to publish books that are accessible, constructive and that challenge accepted opinion, both that of academia and the "moral majority."

Our books are available in all good English language bookstores worldwide. If you don't see the book on the shelves ask the bookstore to order it for you, quoting the ISBN number and title. Alternatively you can order online (all major online retail sites carry our titles) or contact the distributor in the relevant country, listed on the copyright page.

See our website **www.o-books.net** for a full list of over 500 titles, growing by 100 a year.

And tune in to myspiritradio.com for our book review radio show, hosted by June-Elleni Laine, where you can listen to the authors discussing their books.